THE DOG LOVER'S LIBRARY

Edited by *CLIFFORD L. B. HUBBARD*

THE ENGLISH SPRINGER SPANIEL HANDBOOK

THE DOG LOVER'S LIBRARY

Edited by

CLIFFORD L. B. HUBBARD

A series of breed handbooks each written by an authority of general or specialist repute, and copiously illustrated with engravings, prints and photographs of important early and modern dogs. Each book is an up-to-date monograph on a particular breed or variety. Crown octavo, illustrated, 7s. 6d. net.

Other titles include

THE DACHSHUND HANDBOOK
THE STAFFORDSHIRE BULL TERRIER HANDBOOK
THE BOXER HANDBOOK
THE AFGHAN HOUND HANDBOOK
THE COCKER SPANIEL HANDBOOK
THE PEKINGESE HANDBOOK
THE SCOTTISH TERRIER HANDBOOK
THE PEMBROKESHIRE CORGI HANDBOOK
THE CARDIGANSHIRE CORGI HANDBOOK
THE WHIPPET HANDBOOK
THE DALMATIAN HANDBOOK
THE BORZOI HANDBOOK
THE GOLDEN RETRIEVER HANDBOOK
THE BULL TERRIER HANDBOOK
THE BULLMASTIFF HANDBOOK
THE ENGLISH SETTER HANDBOOK
THE BULLDOG HANDBOOK
THE CAIRN TERRIER HANDBOOK
THE PUG HANDBOOK
THE WIRE-HAIRED FOX TERRIER HANDBOOK
THE PAPILLON HANDBOOK
THE DANDIE DINMONT TERRIER HANDBOOK
THE BEAGLE HANDBOOK
THE WELSH TERRIER HANDBOOK
THE YORKSHIRE TERRIER HANDBOOK
THE BLOODHOUND HANDBOOK
THE BASSET HOUND HANDBOOK
THE SHETLAND SHEEPDOG HANDBOOK

SHOOTING FLYING

Frontispiece: [*Canis Dog Features*

'Shooting Flying', from Richard Blome's *Gentleman's Recreation*, 1686.

THE
ENGLISH SPRINGER
SPANIEL
HANDBOOK

GIVING THE ORIGIN AND HISTORY OF THE BREED, ITS
SHOW CAREER, ITS POINTS AND BREEDING

BY

MARY C. SCOTT

NICHOLSON & WATSON

LONDON

First published in 1960

© The Dog Lover's Library, 1960

Printed in GREAT BRITAIN
by
LOVE & MALCOMSON, LTD.
London and Redhill

PREFACE

THE English Springer Spaniel could well be called the 'all-rounder' of the Gundog breeds: as a pal he is affectionate, intelligent and always anxious to please; as a show dog he is attractive and well-mannered; and as a Gundog he is unsurpassed—indeed he will hunt no matter how thick the cover, retrieve and do all that is asked of him.

In this book I have outlined a little of his history and, although so much more could perhaps have been said about many other winning dogs both past and present, in the limited space I have available I have at least been able to mention the leaders—I apologize to the owners and breeders of the many good dogs who, although not Champions, still do much to maintain the present high standard of the breed, and for whom this handbook simply could not find space.

My thanks are due to the Editor, Mr. Clifford Hubbard, for his help and encouragement in this, my first attempt at putting my thoughts and memories into book form; to the Kennel Club for the valuable information derived from the *Stud Book*; to Mr. Frank Warner Hill and Mr. Reg Kelland, who, in spite of their superior knowledge of the breed, did not scoff at my humble efforts but gave me so much good advice. Thanks too, to my many friends who allowed me to publish illustrations of their dogs . . . I only wish many more could have been included.

My final word of thanks is due to the English Springer Spaniel himself, for all the fun and happiness he has given me for so many years, for the many friends he has helped me to make, and for inspiring me to portray his story.

Mary C. Scott.

Bramhope, *June*, 1959.

CONTENTS

CHAPTER   PAGE

  I. ORIGIN AND HISTORY 1

  II. EARLY SHOW DOGS 13

  III. CONTEMPORARY DOGS 30

  IV. THE STANDARD 48
Scale of Points—American Points

  V. BREEDING 54
Mating—Whelping—Docking and Dew-claws

  VI. FEEDING 62
Adult Feeding—Weaning—Puppy Feeding

  VII. GENERAL MANAGEMENT 66
Kennelling—Grooming—Ailments—
Medicine Cupboard

  VIII. EXHIBITING 73
Show Requisites

  IX. TRAINING 78
Obedience Work—Field Work—Qualifying
Certificate

  X. GLOSSARY OF TERMS 84

  XI. BREED CLUBS 91

  XII. TABLE OF REGISTRATIONS FROM 1919-1958 . 93
Whelping Table
Index

ILLUSTRATIONS

Frontispiece ' Shooting Flying ', from Richard Blome's
Gentleman's Recreation, 1686.

Facing page

PLATE I 6
Photograph by the Editor of the actual folding table
of breeds in the rare first book on dogs, Caius' *De
Canibus Britannicis*, 1570. Note the ' Spainel ' and
' Waterspainel ' marked by an added arrow.

PLATE II 7
An excellent early painting of a Springer by Sartorius,
of about 1795: An engraving by John Scott after
Philip Reinagle, first published in 1804.

PLATE III 22
A brace springing a cock pheasant, from Blakey's
Shooting, 1854: A photograph of the coloured
plate ' The Spaniel ' in the Editor's copy of Sydenham Edwards' *Cynographia Britannica*, the plate
dated 1st January, 1801.

PLATE IV 23
Six related breeds from Germany, France, Holland,
England and Brittany. Top left and right: Wachtel-
hund and Picard; centre left and right: Drentsche
Patrijshond and Norfolk Spaniel; bottom left and
right: Pont Audemer and the Breton Spaniel.

PLATE V 38
Maud Earl's beautiful painting of "Tissington
Flush": Two Norfolks from Shaw's *Illustrated
Book of the Dog*, 1879-80: B. Smith's engraving
after a painting by Stubbs.

Facing page

PLATE VI 39
    F. Winton Smith's Ch. "Beechgrove Donaldson", about 1905: H. S. Lloyd's Ch. "Springbok of Ware": The bitch Ch. "Inveresk Coronation", born 1923.

PLATE VII 54
    Six influential Springers in chronological order. Top left and right: Ch. "Peter of Lorton Fell" and Int. Ch. "Advert of Solway"; centre left and right: "St. Peter's Victoria" and "Peter's Benefactor"; bottom left and right: Ch. "Bramhope Recorder" and Ch. "Duchess of Stubham".

PLATE VIII 55
    Ch. "Stokeley Lucky": Ch. "Stokeley Bonny Boy": Int. Ch. "Frejax Royal Salute".

PLATE IX 62
    Mr. I. Davies with Ch. "Clintonhouse George": Ch. "Camdin Chief": Sh. Ch. "Wallburn Wallflower".

PLATES X & XI . . . . 62 & 63
    "Showman of Shotton" (left) and Am. Ch. "Melilotus Royal Oak" (below): "Northdown Donna" (right) and "Boxer of Bramhope" (below.)

PLATE XII 63
    Top left: Am. Ch. "Kaintuck Beau Brummel"; centre left: Int. Ch. "Ascot's Ajax"; bottom left: Sh. Ch. "Studley Brave Buccaneer"; top right: Sh. Ch. "Beauvallet of Crosslane"; bottom right: Ch. "Stokeley Gay Boy".

PLATE XIII 70
    Sh. Ch. "Vanity Fair of Stubham": Sh. Ch. "Stokeley Sea Sprite": Ch. "Mowgrain Mr. Chips".

Facing page

PLATE XIV 71
    The Author with her Ch. " Bathsheba of Bram-
hope ": Miss Anne Beattie with Ch. " Belarosa of
Bramhope ": Ch. " Bathsheba of Bramhope ", Mrs.
Gwen Broadley (judge), Mr. Reg Kelland (president), and Ch. " Inveresk Raider ".

PLATE XV 86
    Sh. Ch. "Hazel of Stubham ": Am. Ch. " Meli-
lotus Shooting Star ": Ch. " Alexander of Stubham ".

PLATE XVI 87
    Sh. Ch. " Grand Lodge " (above left) and Mrs.
Frankish with Ch. " Colmaris Chancellor ": Mrs.
E. Beale and a litter by her " Racedale Rover ".

CHAPTER I

ORIGIN AND HISTORY

ALL through the ages man has loved to hunt with a dog as his companion, and doubtless the original 'Springer' earned his name through his ability to spring the game for his master.

The exact country of origin of the English Springer Spaniel is unknown, but it is likely that the first dogs of the breed came here from the Continent, probably from Spain, as the name ' Spaniel ' (also spelled ' Spaynel ' or ' Spainel ' in earlier times) implies.

In manuscript writings of about the close of the fourteenth century, Gaston de Foix, a powerful and rich lord of southern France, author of *Le Livre de Chasse* and a warrior famous for his hunting feats, described their work, quartering in front of the master, flushing game and retrieving from land and water—all very like the work of modern Springer Spaniels. This great sportsman is said at times to have had (at least according to Froissart's *Chronicles*) as many as 1,600 trained hunting dogs in his kennels at one time—just imagine feeding and looking after that little lot! Food and labour must indeed have been cheap and plentiful in those days.

About 1570, Dr. Caius, physician to King Edward VI, described in his *De Canibus Britannicis* what he

1

called a land Spaniel, as distinct from a water Spaniel.*
And about 1638 Ulysses Aldrovandus wrote in his
natural history work, *Quadrupedibus, of a* ' Spaniel dog
with floppy ears, the chest, belly, and feet white, picked
out with black, the rest of the body black '.

In 1621 was published Gervase Markham's *Hungers
Prevention: Or, The Whole Arte Of Fowling By Water
and Land*, one of the rarest of his books.† In it he men-
tions the Water Spaniel and the Land Spaniel, which
latter he divides into the Crouching Spaniel and the
Springing Spaniel, both being of the same stock. He then
subdivided the Springer Spaniel into two sizes and called
the smaller one the Cocking Spaniel.

Markham speaks well of the Land Spaniel. So well
that I yield to the temptation to quote this quaint passage
(exactly as it was printed) from the first edition of his
little book:

> Yet is their none so excellent indeede as the true
> bred Land-Spaniell, being of a nimble and good
> size, rather small then grosse, and of a
> couragious and fierie mettall, evermore loving
> and desiring toyle, when toyle seems most

---

* John Caius, co-founder of Gonville and Caius College, Cam-
bridge, was Master of the College from 1559 to 1573, when he died.
He was successively Court physician to Edward VI, Mary, and Eliza-
beth I, and as friend of Queen Elizabeth he undoubtedly gained
unrivalled information concerning the sporting dogs of his time in
Britain. His Latin work on British dogs was freely translated into
English in 1576 by Abraham Fleming and published as *Of Englishe
Dogges*: both works are excessively rare to-day. For further informa-
tion see Chapter III, 'Dr. Caius' Contribution' in *The Literature of
British Dogs*, Ponterwyd, 1949.

† See *The Literature of British Dogs*, Ponterwyd, 1949, Chapter
IV, ' Turberville and Markham '.

yrksome and wearie, which although you cannot know in a whelpe so yong, as it is intended he must be, when you first begin to traine him to this purpose, yet may you have a strong speculation therein, if you choose him from a right litter or breede, wherein by succession you have knowne that the whole generation have been endued with all these qualities, as namely; that he is a strong, lusty and nimble raundger, both of active foote, wanton tayle, and busie nostrill, that his toyle is without wearinesse, his search without changeablenesse, and yet, that no delight nor desire transport him beyond feare or obedience; for it is the perfectest charracter of the most perfectest Spaniel, ever to be fearefull and loving to him that is his Master and keeper.

The above passage is only part of one long sentence running over pp. 266-267 of *Hungers Prevention* . . . surely one of the 'most perfectest' praises of a Spaniel's working character!

By the year 1800, Spaniels had begun to be divided into two groups. Dogs weighing up to 25 lb. were called Cockers or Cocking Spaniels, because they were used for woodcock, and the larger dogs weighing around 45 lb. were called Field Spaniels or English Spaniels.

By the year 1812, a pure strain of English Springers was beginning: " Mop I ", bred by the Boughey family of Aqualate in Shropshire, although rather Clumberish, and with a coat inclined to be curly, was of true Springer type. In those days Norfolk was a great sporting county, and liver-and-white and black-and-white Spaniels were much in demand. A much criticised dog was " Tissington Flush " owned by Sir Hugo Fitz-Herbert, a dog who was

exhibited as a Norfolk Spaniel around 1857. " Flush "
a rather high on the leg liver-and-white, was said to have
had the head of an English Setter and was described by
James Farrow as ' just what a ' Setter man ' would like '!
Later the 'Tissington' Springers became famous all
over the country.

Incidentally, the so-called Norfolk Spaniel appears to
have had no connection with the Dukes of Norfolk. In
a very long letter to the Editor of the *Kennel Gazette* (of
December, 1899, pages 512-3) James Farrow, the
great Cocker Spaniel breeder, wrote '. . . as far back as
1845 Youatt, writing about Spaniels, says the breed was
brought into notice by the late Duke of Norfolk. A few
years ago I tried to bottom the alleged connection between the so called Norfolk Spaniel and the Norfolk
family, and the following is a copy of a letter I have in
my possession from the Duke of Norfolk on the subject:

> I have never myself heard of the Norfolk
> Spaniel, or of any special interest for them on the
> part of our family. I have heard, however, that
> the Duke of Norfolk at the beginning of the pre-
> sent century, who was the cousin and prede-
> cessor of my great grandfather, had a breed of
> Sussex Spaniels of which he was very fond.
>
> I have heard that the Sussex Spaniel is a breed
> which still exists.

After reading the above facts I think you will come to
the conclusion I have had for years—that the Norfolk
Spaniel is a myth and a delusion.'

And yet James Watson gave the Norfolk Spaniel
(myth or not) a special section in volume I of his *The
Dog Book*, London, 1906—although *he* says that the

Duke's own dogs were 'Toy Black and Tan' Spaniels. It appears then that there is rather more (or is it less?) than meets the eye in the Norfolk matter.

In *The Complete Farrier, and British Sportsman,* 1816, Richard Lawrence described what he called the 'Water-dog', and said of it (p. 405) 'During his puppyhood, this dog displays a strong inclination to be busy; he takes delight in removing shoes, boots, mops, brooms, pattens, etc.' Any reader owning a lovable, mischievous Springer puppy will realize that habits haven't changed much since 1816!

Richard Lawrence, who was a veterinary surgeon of long experience with dogs, also had something to say of the Springer in his book just referred to, and began his chapter on 'The Springer and Cock-Spaniel' with the following paragraph:

> This race of dogs consists of two kinds, one of which being considerably larger than the other, is known by the appellation of the springer, or springing-spaniel, as applicable to every kind of game; the smaller is called the cocker, or cock-spaniel, it being more particularly adapted to covert, or woodcock shooting.

He then described in detail the two breeds and even referred briefly to the Sussex Spaniel before dealing with the working and training of Spaniels generally. His description of the English Springer sounds a trifle quaint to-day perhaps but was certainly an apt one considering it was written close upon a century and a half ago. The following is quoted verbatim from p. 401:

> The true English springer differs but little in

figure from the setter, except in size; varying only in a small degree, if any, from a red yellow, or liver colour, or white, which seems to be the invariable external standard of this breed; and, being nearly two fifths less in height and strength than the setter, delicately formed, ears long, soft, and pliable, coat waving and silky, eyes and nose red or black, the tail somewhat bushy and pendulous, and always in motion when actively employed.

The Spaniel Club was formed in 1885 by a few gentlemen who drew up Standards of points for the various Spaniel breeds to try to help breeders to breed to a specified type. A Mr. T. B. Bowers of Chester was at that time recognized as a leading authority on the Spaniel. Even in those days difference of opinion arose between the show bench advocates and the sporting gentlemen, and to counteract the craze for 'fancy' points the Spaniel Club thought of holding Field Trials. This brought a rival club into being, viz., the Sporting Spaniel Society. On the 3rd of January, 1899, this society held a working trial at Sutton Scarsdale on the estate of Mr. William Arkwright (the author of that great work *The Pointer and his Predecessors*, 1902), and later in the same year, on the 12th of December, another trial was held at Little Green, Havant, on Mr. B. J. Warwick's estate. The records do not show that a Springer was in the awards, but, of course, at that date Springers had no separate classification, and the winner, Mr. Hearnshaw's " Burton Duchess " was just described as a liver-and-white Spaniel bitch.

It is thought that about 1812 or 1815 the English Springer was imported into the United States of

Plate I

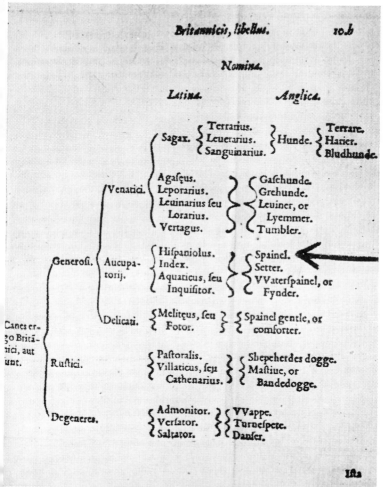

Britannicis, libellus.   10.b

Nomina.

Latina.   Anglica.

Sagax. { Terrarius.
         Leuerarius.   } Hunde. { Terrare.
         Sanguinarius.   Harier.
                                    Bludhunde.

Venatici. { Agaseus.   { Gasehunde.
            Leporarius.   Grehunde.
            Leuinarius seu   Leuiner, or
            Lorarius.   Lyemmer.
            Vertagus.   Tumbler.

Generosi. Aucupa- { Hispaniolus.   { Spainel.
          torij.   Index.   Setter.
                    Aquaticus, seu   VVaterspainel, or
                    Inquisitor.   Fynder.

Canes er- Delicati. { Meliteus, seu { Spainel gentle, or
go Britá-   Fotor.   comforter.
nici, aut
unt.   Rustici. { Pastoralis.   { Shepeherdes dogge.
                      Villaticus, seu   Mastiue, or
                      Cathenarius.   Bandedogge.

           Degeneres. { Admonitor.   { VVappe.
                        Versator.   Turnespete.
                        Saltator.   Danser.

                                              Ista

Canis Dog Features.

Photograph by the Editor of the actual folding table of breeds in the rare first book on dogs, Caius' *De Canibus Britannicis*, 1570. Note the 'Spaniel' and 'Waterspainel' marked by an added arrow.

Plate II

Courtesy Gerald Massey.

An excellent early painting of a Springer by Sartorius, of about 1795.

Canis Dog Features.

An engraving by John Scott after Philip Reinagle,
first published in 1804.

America, but it was not until 1886 that they were shown at the New York Fancier's Show at Madison Square Garden, New York, where " Dash II ", an imported Norfolk Spaniel caused much comment.

In 1902, the Kennel Club granted a separate place in their *Stud Book* for the English Springer Spaniel, and a separate classification at their show in 1903, where Mr. William Arkwright judged the breed and awarded the dog Challenge Certificate to Mr. Winton Smith's " Beechgrove Will ", with Mr. Harry Jones' bitch, " Fansome ", Best Opposite Sex. By 1906 " Beechgrove Will " became the breed's first Champion. At this time, apart from the Aqualate strain, the Springers were of mixed origin, and provided they looked like Springers they were registered as such! For instance a Welsh Cocker, " Corrin of Gerwin " (*K.C.S.B.* I, 13931F), a very well-known dog, later became known as " Corrin of Gerwn " (*K.C.S.B.* 894G), Welsh Springer! His son, " Guy of Gerwn " was registered as a Springer; and a black-white-and-tan daughter of the famous " Beechgrove Will " was registered as a Field Spaniel!

As I have already said, 1906 was the year in which the breed's first Champion, Ch. " Beechgrove Will ", was made up. Well that year was also to see published what became one of the most important books in the English language on Spaniels. Its principal author was a gentleman known well to me—the late Mr. C. A. Phillips of Dildawn, Castle Douglas, and a great authority on Springers. The book was, of course, that well-known classic, *The Sporting Spaniel*, 1906, written by Mr. Phillips and Mr. R. Claude Cane . . . a work most carefully written and copiously illustrated.

I shall always treasure the memory of the talks Mr. Phillips and I had by the fire in the library of his lovely old house, his desk piled high with papers and books, none of which was allowed to be moved by any other hand than his; he could lay his hand on any paper for reference and had such a wonderful memory right to the end of his days.

I remember him describing a painting he had seen in Antwerp by Jan Steen, entitled 'A Flemish Wedding Feast', dated 1626; in the foreground was a lovely liver-white-and-tan Spaniel of Springer type. Few of the old pictures depicted this colour—indeed most show them as liver, yellow or red mixed with white. To-day, of course, any other colour than liver-and-white, black-and-white, or either with tan markings, would be frowned upon. I still treasure a copy of *The Sporting Spaniel* given to me by Mr. Phillips.

The newly formed Sporting Spaniel Society was incurring a certain amount of bitter feeling among the members of the older Spaniel Club, and I quote from Mr. Phillips' book: 'Several prominent members of the new club freely accused old breeders of Show Spaniels of having used Dachshund and Beagle crosses, to procure length of body and shortness of leg, but as they could quote no specific cases as proof of these charges, they were generally discredited and fell to the ground'. At this time there was much heated correspondence in the leading canine papers on this subject and rumour was rife. That fine old sporting parson, Mr. Daniel, was one who strongly condemned such crosses, as he stated that it bred a love of hare-hunting into the breed.

All this was before I was born, but whispers and rumours were still around in my early days in Springers, and when one sees 'Settery' and 'Pointer' heads, 'Cockerish' ears, etc., perhaps one may be forgiven for wondering 'why' and 'how'? Perhaps, one day, further light may be shed on this subject, and breeding secrets of the early twentieth century may be published. I, for one, am grateful to these pioneers of the past, for through the years has evolved the handsome and intelligent Springer we all know and love to-day.

Up to 1903 there were few exhibitors in the breed. *Kennel Club Stud Book* records show the chief exhibitors at that time to be Sir Hugo Fitz-Herbert and Messrs. W. Arkwright, H. Jones, C. Watts, I. Sharpe, and F. Winton Smith.

Around 1900, the late Mr. C. C. Eversfield of Denne Park, Horsham, was winning at trials with two dogs registered as Field Spaniels, called " Brownie " and " Shultz ". After these he had a succession of Trial winners in "Nimrod ", " Canonite Powder ", " Nitro Powder " and " Diamond Powder ". His most famous dog was " Velox Powder ", whose pedigree was pure Aqualate, and could be traced in an unbroken line back to 1812. This dog began his winning career at trials in 1904 and continued to run right up to 1912—in all these years he never ran unplaced! It is written that this very intelligent dog was able to act as ' teacher ' to the young Springers at Denne Park, and if any of the young ' hopefuls ' attempted to run in when sent for a retrieve, he would catch hold of their ears or collars. He was one of the early Field Trial Champions.

Sitting round the fireside at Bramhope I have listened by the hour to the tales of the late Mr. William East— ' Bill ' East, as he was known to all of us who had the pleasure of knowing and loving this grand old man. ' Arkwright ' and ' Eversfield ' were household names to him, and he knew his countryside, Somerset and the Mendip Hills, like the back of his hand.

I once copied several of his poems, which he was fond

of reciting, his head back in the armchair, a small
Scotch at his elbow, after a day out on the moors with
the dogs and the guns. Of all the places in the world, I
think the place he loved best was the little village of
Tetton where he had spent so many years, and I know
he would like my readers to have before them his little
tribute ' To Tetton ':

Dear Tetton snugly nestling at the foot of the hills,
Thy beauty enchants us and fills us with thrills.
Mid the oaks and the pines, the beech and the limes,
The yew trees and hollies of ancient times.
In your gardens and park where you look o'er the vale,
Away to the Mendips o'er hill and o'er dale,
Not many are privileged to live 'mid such beauty.
That surrounds thee, all around thee, dear Tetton.

Then away at the back up the green rolling hill.
To Buncombe and Ball where the song birds trill,
And the primroses peep at the spring of the year,
To make a white carpet for the wild red deer.
Where the hinds and their calves with soft limpid eyes
Graze mid bluebells and fern, which doth arise,
From their long winter's sleep 'neath the hazel and ash
Where the fallow deer love to gambol and dash.
And the buzzard soars high o'er Broomfield's steep sides
Where the red fox lurks, and cunningly hides.
Then on the way home you go over the top
When the Brendons and Blackdowns will surely cry ' stop '!
While you gaze o'er the vale so peaceful and green,
Was ever in England a more lovely scene?
Truly privileged are we to live mid such beauty,
That surrounds thee, all around thee, dear Tetton.

In later years when he retired, he became well known as a judge both at shows and Field Trials, and his unfailing kindness and gentleness to both dogs and exhibitors is something I shall always remember; truly he was one of ' nature's gentlemen ', and a well-loved character in the English Springer world.

In the early part of this present century there is no doubt that Mr. Eversfield was the largest breeder of Springers. After his untimely death in 1915, nearly all his kennel was sold by auction at Aldridge's. Forty-one Springers realized 983 guineas, a small fortune in those ' good old days '! Another good Field Trial kennel at that time was at Hagley, owned by Mr. J. P. Gardner. His best dog was one called, simply, " Tring ".

About this time, Mr. C. A. Phillips (' Rivington ') decided to develop his own strain of Springers; he bred an over-size Cocker* bitch to a local working Springer dog, and out of this mating came his successful F.T. Ch. " Rivington Sam ", who competed successfully with the great " Denne Duke " and other Champions from the famous kennels of Mr. Eversfield. The First World War put an end to " Sam "s career as a Field Trial winner, but he has left his mark in the breed through his grandson F. T. Ch. " Rex of Avendale " who appears way back in many of our present-day pedigrees. ' Avendale ' was the prefix of the Duke of Hamilton and Brandon.

The first known import under the formal name of English Springer Spaniel to the United States was in 1907, when Mr. Ernest Wells imported two for Mr.

---

* For further particulars of Mr. Phillips' life work in Spaniels see *The Cocker Spaniel Handbook*, 1951, in this series, by Nesta M. Basnett Broughall.—*Editor.*

Robert Dumont of Morristown, New Jersey. Gradually the English Springer became more and more popular in America as a working dog, although it was not until 1924 that the English Springer Spaniel Field Trial Association was formed.

CHAPTER II

DURING the First World War breeding activities were cut down to a minimum—from 1914-1918 the sporting fraternity were actively engaged on both sides of the English Channel with far bigger game than pheasants, partridge and the humble rabbit! In fact only twenty-eight Springers were registered at the Kennel Club during the whole of 1917, but things started looking up by 1919 and registrations jumped to seventy-one. The Spaniel Club Field Trials were held on 3rd December, 1919, with the Duke of Hamilton and Brandon's " Rex of Avendale " winning the first prize.

In 1920 many of the big championship shows started again, and English Springers were classified once more on 6th and 7th October, at the Edinburgh (Scottish Kennel Club) championship show, where Mr. D. McDonald's " Little Brand " won the dog C.C., and Mr. L. Turton Price's " Horsford Honeybell " won the bitch C.C. The only other show in 1920 to classify the breed was that held at the Crystal Palace by the Kennel Club, where once again Mr. McDonald took top honours with " Little Brand " winning the dog C.C., and his " Little Sunray " the bitch C.C.

By 1924 things were almost back to normal, and no less than fifteen championship shows classified English Springers. I do not want to bore my readers with lists of dead and gone winners, but would like to recall some of the many famous breeders of those days, and I feel that the simplest and most interesting way to do this will be giving a brief note about each of the early prefixes in alphabetical order.

I have already mentioned the **Avendale** strain, owned by the Duke of Hamilton and Brandon. These famous dogs were handled then by Mr. Tom Gaunt, still as active as ever to-day with Lady Howe's kennel of Labrador Retrievers. Dual Ch. "Flint of Avendale" was one of the three Dual Champions ever bred.

Banchory—the prefix of Lorna, Countess Howe is best known to-day among Labrador and Pug (see Mrs. W. Swainston Goodger's *The Pug Handbook*, 1959) breeders, but in the 1920's Lady Howe owned many great Springers. The most famous of them was F.T. Ch. "Banchory Bright", a bitch combining the 'Rivington', 'Avendale', and 'Denne' strains on both sides of her pedigree. She was six times a Field Trial Champion, winner of thirty-three Stakes, including the Spaniel championship twice, and the brace and team championship stakes in 1926 and 1927.

In the U.S.A. in 1931, "Banchory Flame", owned by Dr. and Mrs. Samuel Millbank, became a Field Trial Champion. "Flame" was by "Fireflash" out of "Banchory Gloss".

Beauchief—the prefix of the one and only Frank Warner Hill, my Guide, Philosopher and Friend; since winning my first ever Challenge Certificate under him with "Boxer of Bramhope", I have always looked to him for advice and he has been unfailingly helpful and taught me so much about the Springer and other breeds from the great fount of his knowledge.

His first Springer came from Alfreton Hall in Derbyshire, and cost the princely sum of £5! She was registered as " Beauchief Lady Barbara ", and was the foundation of the kennel. Mated to Mr. H. S. Lloyd's Int. Ch. " Jambok of Ware ", she produced the well-known " Beauchief Major " and " Beauchief Nicholas " in her first litter. To continue the line Mr. Hill scoured Derbyshire again, in those days extremely strong in the breed, and once more expended £5 on a wild little bitch bought at a remote keeper's cottage in the highest part of Derbyshire, the Cat and Fiddle Inn, and introduced to him by that great character, Mr. Ellis Ashton, former head keeper to the Duke of Devonshire and owner of the famous ' Leecroft ' Flat-coated Retrievers. This bitch's pedigree seemed somewhat sketchy, but was as reliable as the pedigrees of the famous Derbyshire working Sheepdogs, who in those days had no stud records, but whose pedigrees were carried down in the minds of the shepherds! This little bitch whose pedigree consisted mostly of kennel names only, also contained the name of one very reputable sire, " Sam of Hagley ". She was bought on this unrecorded but accurate breeding to carry on the bloodline of " Lady Barbara " through " Beauchief Nicholas ".

From the start of the search to the result took two years and resulted in two Champions in her first litter, Ch. " Beauchief Buchanan ", the F.T. winner and Ch. " Beauchief Bonnetta "; she in turn produced the famous Ch. " Beauchief Benefactor ", who was the first Springer bred and owned in this country to go Best in Show all breeds at a championship show. I trust I have worded this claim to fame correctly, for previously Mr. A. McNab Chassels had won the highest honours at Cruft's with his superb bitch, Ch. " Inveresk Coronation "; the owners are agreed on these two as the best brace we have produced and they greatly resembled each other on all the principal points which go to form our conception of the perfect English Springer Spaniel.

About the period of "Major" and "Nicholas" appeared another fine Springer bred by Mr. Victor Blake of Ashbourne, named "Standard", who, sold to Mr. George Taylor of the 'Carnfield' prefix, became a great winning Champion and was eventually exported to India. About the time of "Benefactor" the tables were turned and a dog bred in India by H. H. the Maharajah of Patiala, out of an exported bitch famous as a brood, but not herself a Champion, "Sidger", mated in India to another exported dog produced "Caliph of Malwa". Unbeaten as a Champion in India, he was sent to Britain into the care of Mr. H. S. Lloyd, and he eventually became a Champion here. I am greatly indebted to Mr. Warner Hill for the above information.

Beechgrove—owned by Mr. F. Winton Smith, I have already mentioned in Chapter I, see page 7.

Boghurst—owned by Major H. E. C. Doyne-Ditmas, whose "Boghurst Carlo" and "Boghurst Rover" were winning well in 1923. The dog I remember best was Ch. "Boghurst Bristle" owned by Mr. McNab Chassels; so well remembered possibly because my husband owned his litter sister, "Boghurst Berry" way back in 1928.

Bryngarw—owned by Capt. O. P. Traherne, who was for many years a president of the English Springer Spaniel Club and a great advocate of the Springer. Handled by Mr. W. Church, his strain made its presence felt at Field Trials around 1924. His F.T. Chs. "Bryngarw Coleraine", "Jock", "Firefly", "Firearm" and "Firelight" won many stakes. He was well known in

America where he was invited to judge the American Field Trial championship.

Carnfield—owned by Mr. George Taylor, that great veteran of the breed. If only he could be persuaded to write his memoirs in that elegant hand-writing of his, what an interest to breeders they would be! " Carnfield King " was one of the best known of his early winners; " Carnfield Cadet " and " Carnfield Lily " won C.Cs. in 1927, and he is one of the few breeders of that era who will also appear in my chapter on contemporary dogs— truly a great record!

Dalshangan—owned by Mr. A. L. Trotter, a Scottish sportsman, who owned the great F.T. Ch. " Dalshangan Dandy Boy ". This Springer did much for the breed in siring many good dogs and F.T. winners both here and in the U.S.A., where in 1929 a dog called " Tedwyns Trex ", sired by " Dandy Boy ", became a Field Trial Champion, and won his championship on the bench in 1930.

Denne—owned by Mr. C. C. Eversfield, already listed among the pioneers of the early days in my preceding chapter, see pages 9 and 11.

Downton—owned by Sir W. Rouse Boughton, Bart., a great supporter of Field Trials. His dogs also won on the show bench; " Downton Darkie ", and " Downton Duchess " and " Tinker " were all well known in the 1920's. He also bred the famous " Dalshangan Dandy Boy ", known originally as " Downton Flash ", who was born in 1921 and later owned by Mr. Trotter. In those days the Kennel Club allowed the new owner to give a complete change of name if desired, now, of course it is only permissible to add the new owner's prefix or suffix, and this is only allowed if the dog has not qualified for inclusion in the *Kennel Club Stud Book*. I think this is a very sensible ruling, as in this way the breeder still retains a certain amount of the honour and glory of having bred a dog who may become famous in other hands.

of Harting—was Lt. Col. F. B. H. Carrell's well-known suffix. Around 1927 he was winning well with " Georgina of Harting " and " Groompy ", and then in 1930 " Honour " and " Rollick " were winning Certificates. After the Second World War when beaters were scarce, his team of working Springers was much in demand in the New Forest area at very eminent shoots and became quite famous. I never saw them working myself, but understand it was quite a sight to see this large team beating the undergrowth in the forest to Col. Carrell's orders. Dual Ch. " Thoughtful of Harting " was perhaps his best known Springer—one of the very few Dual Champions ever bred.

Hemlington—owned by Mr. A. W. Carter, breeder of the famous " Hemlington Kalgar ". Sired by Mr. H. S. Lloyd's " Springbok of Ware ", " Kalgar " was sold to the Hon. Mrs. Quintin Dick (now Lorna Countess Howe), and did a lot of winning in the 1920's. I am glad to say that Mr. Carter still retains his interest in the breed and his prefix is still in the awards at our present-day shows.

Higham—owned by Miss C. M. Francis, one of our great sporting ladies of the breed, equally at home in the show ring or at Field Trials. Miss Francis owns that lovely bitch Ch. " Higham Teal ", who made her name in the early 1930's and later produced Ch. " Higham Tom Tit ", afterwards sold to Mrs. W. Selby-Lowndes.

(Lady Angela Lambe). " Teal " produced many well-known winners including " Higham Ticket ", " Higham Thyme ", and several other good ones. At the time of writing Miss Francis is very active as the chairman of the English Springer Spaniel Club, is an enthusiastic supporter of Field Trials, and a popular exhibitor and judge at championship shows.

Highedge—owned by Mr. Morrel of Derbyshire, is one of the smaller kennels. However it is one which has had a lasting influence on the breed from the early 1930's when his " Betty of Highedge " mated to that prolific sire Ch. " Beauchief Benefactor ", produced many good ones like " Highedge Keeper ", " Minnie ", and others. Indeed many of to-day's winners show " Betty " way back in their pedigrees.

Horsford—owned by Mr. William Humphrey. Here we have another truly great sportsman, a colourful raconteur, and one whose stories told round a blazing fire in the hotel bar after a Field Trial, have often kept me up until daybreak! His yarns would fill many books, although it would be difficult to capture his dry humour, as with a twinkling eye he would tell of the tame otter that slept in his bed (yes, I said *in* not on, believe it or not)! Of the golden eagle with its enormous wing span, strong enough to break a man's leg, which he tamed and taught to hunt foxes on the wild hills around his lovely home in Shropshire. His coats were padded on the shoulder and this great bird would perch there, or on the back of his chair at mealtimes, and on the foot of his bed while he slept. His skill in falconry is uncanny,* but

---

* William Humphrey contributed a special section on the use of trained Field Trial dogs working with peregrines, falcons and tiercel (and had much to say of Field Trials generally) in Clifford Hubbard's *The English Setter Handbook*, 1958, in this series.—*Editor.*

then, I understand his ancestors came over as falconers with William the Conqueror, so this is born and bred in him. Many were the wonderful Springers he bred and trained, most famous of all being Dual Ch. " Horsford Hetman ", a good looking and great working dog, one of the only three Dual Champions of that time.

Inveresk—owned by Mr. A. McNab Chassels, D.L., J.P., who has been described as the ' Father of the Scottish Kennel Club committee '. He is indeed a man of many parts—hotel keeper, food and wine expert, internationally famous judge of dogs and horses, and one whose great charm and personality would make him a success in any sphere. Only recently he scored a huge success as a B.B.C. commentator at the Scottish Kennel Club's championship show, held in Kelvin Hall, Glasgow. As a Convener of the Scottish Kennel Club he was asked about various breeds of dogs and staggered the powers that be by launching out into ' The Twa Dugs ' by Rabbie Burns! As a television personality he proved to be a ' natural ', urbane, knowledgeable, witty and wise.

His sense of humour is superb. He told me of an incident that happened some years ago: as provost, he was visiting a mental hospital. The superintendent was out, and he was being shown round by a small dark man. Taking his leave, Mr. Chassels said, ' You know, I don't think I've introduced myself, I'm the provost of Coatbridge '. ' Ach ', said the wee man, patting him comfortingly, ' They'll soon put that notion oot o' your heid. When I came in at first I was convinced I was Napoleon '. Then he added ' Now I'm no' that sure '!

Best known dog of all his Springers was Ch. " Inveresk Chancellor ", well known both here and in America. A black-and-white bred by Miss R. Pike in 1925, he was originally named " Dilkusha Punch ". He was sired by Mr. H. S. Lloyd's " Jamson of Ware ", he later went to Mr. H. J. Placey of Quebec and became a Triple International Champion. My very first personal memory of Mr. McNab Chassels is of 1946, when he judged the first open show for the breed to be held after the war. Mrs. H. Howard of the ' Chastleton ' Springers was then honorary secretary of the Midland English Springer Spaniel Society, and to her must go the honour of organising such a wonderful show with an entry of 337, which, I should think, must be a record for the breed. I was very small fry among the many famous names present that day, and shall never forget the thrill when the then unknown puppy " Boxer of Bramhope " won the cup for Best Puppy bred by exhibitor, the Elom Challenge Cup, and Diploma for Best Puppy in Show— he was then just 7½ months old. How time flies, and yet when I was talking to Mr. McNab Chassels at Cruft's he was as handsome and debonair as ever, and appears never to have altered from this first day I met him!

Laverstoke—owned by Lady Portal. Here we have had a great name in Springers for many many years. "Laverstoke Pilate", "Pancake", "Sapphire", "Pedro", and many others bore this famous prefix, and best known of all, perhaps, were Ch. " Laverstoke Pepper " owned by the Hon. George Scott, and that lovely Ch. " Laverstoke Pattern ".

L'ile—owned by Mr. David McDonald of Dundee, a great breeder and showman for many years. Perhaps his most famous dog was Ch. " Little Brand " who won the first dog C.C. offered after the commencement of championship shows in 1920, and was very soon a full

Champion. "Little Queen", "Little King". Ch. "L'ile Winnie Lass", "L'ile Brown Jack"—many are the famous names that came from this kennel, and all good lookers and good workers. He also owned the famous Ch. "Nuthill Dignity", well known in the U.S.A.

Marmion—was the suffix owned by The Hon. George Scott in the early 1930's. In all probability his greatest dog was Ch. "Marmion of Marmion", a Champion whose name appears in so many of our winning pedigrees of to-day.

Matford—owned by Mr. E. Trimble. Mr. Trimble is well remembered as a judge of the breed but who later devoted his time to judging and committee work for the English Springer Spaniel Club. In the late 1920's his "Shot", "Scamp" and "Sport" were all well-known winners.

Nobel—Mr. R. R. Kelland's famed prefix. One of the founder members of the English Springer Spaniel Club, Mr. Kelland is one who in his time has been secretary, chairman and president of the Club (the two beautiful trophies given by him to the Club will commemorate for all time his great work). Needless to say he is a great authority on the breed, and has bred, trained and exhibited with success at both shows and Field Trials. He is a very dear friend of mine, a great sporting gentleman, a grand shot and handler of a dog, fair and fearless in his judging whether it be at Field Trials or Shows. Blessed with a great sense of humour, and able to take a joke whether it be for or against himself, he never ages and is truly young in heart.

I well remember the consternation at Manchester City championship show a few years ago, where he

Plate III

Canis Dog Features.

A brace springing a cock pheasant,
from Blakey's *Shooting*, 1854.

Canis Dog Features.

A photograph of the coloured plate ' The Spaniel ' in the Editor's copy of Sydenham
Edwards' *Cynographia Britannica*, the plate dated 1st Jan. 1801.

Plate IV

Canis Dog Features.

Six related breeds from Germany, France, Holland, England and Brittany
(*top, left and right*) Wachtelhund and Picard ; (*centre, left and right*) Drentsche
Patrijshond and Norfolk Spaniel ; (*bottom, left and right*) Pont Audemer and the
Breton Spaniel.

was down to judge several Gundog breeds: at well past judging time he had not turned up, calls were continual over the loud speakers but with no success, and eventually somebody else took over his breeds. Telephone calls went to his home, to the mortuary, hospitals and all likely and unlikely places; but it was not until 11 p.m. that same night that he was finally traced, returning from a peaceful night at the cinema! He had been blissfully unaware of all the excitement, as he thought he was due to judge the following day—and turned up one day late! Needless to say he has never heard the last of the one and only slip in his long and distinguished career. [Thank you, Reg, for being such a sport in allowing me to publish this amusing little incident.] "Nobel Standard", winning in the early 1930's, was one of his grand dogs, and his photograph and many others adorn the walls of the sitting-room at his home, Orchard House, Bidford-on-Avon.

Noranby—is, of course, the well-known prefix owned by Mrs. W. M. Charlesworth. Her "Noranby Rusty", "Noranby Rattle", and others winning well at Field Trials in the ownership of Capt. Traherne in 1933, but nowadays her name is associated more with Golden Retrievers . . . and I feel that English Springers lost a valuable supporter when this lady left their ranks!

[According to the *Golden Retriever Handbook*, 1953, by Elma Stonex, Mrs. Charlesworth, herself the author of a book on the Golden Retriever, began in Goldens as long ago as 1906, and is generally regarded as one of the best friends that breed has ever had.—*Editor*.]

Pierrepont—the prefix used by Mr. W. D. Edwards, a Field Trial enthusiast of many years standing. Right from the early days of the 1920's until his death quite recently, Mr. Edwards ran his dogs at nearly every Trial. F. T. Ch. " Pierrepont Splint ", " Pierrepont Brand ", and " Perfection ", were only three of his numerous winners.

Ranscombe—owned by Miss Morland Hooper, a great supporter of our breed for many years, and as actively interested to-day as she was in 1920 when her " Ranger of Ranscombe " was in the awards at the Kennel Club show. Registered as a golden liver-and-white, by " Dash " out of " Bell ", he sired many winners. " Rollick " by Ch. " Little Brand ", was another good one, and in bitches, " Reipple " was a good winner and dam of many winners. In 1927 came " Roan ", " Romp ", " Rascal " and others—the ' of Ranscombes ', were indeed well known—even until the Second World War forced Miss Hooper to cut breeding activities down to a minimum. I shall continue the record of this suffix when I deal with contemporary dogs.

Renrut—the prefix owned by Miss F. L. Turner, and a good dual purpose kennel of the 1930 era. Her dogs were both good lookers and good workers, " Tickie," " Patsy, " " Rosery Brambletyke ", and on to my old " Renrut Rose " by " Renrut Beau " out of " Beauchief Benefactor ", who produced Ch. " Belarosa of Bramhope ", who holds the post-war record for a bitch with fifteen C.Cs. to date under fifteen different judges!

Rivington—was the prefix so widely used by Mr. C. A. Phillips, whom I have already referred to in my first chapter. However, through the 1920's Mr. Phillips' " Rocket ", " Meg ", " Ringlet ", " Don ", " Rollo ", and others too numerous to list were all taking awards at the Field Trials—what a tremendous influence this affix has had on the working Springers for all time!

Roundwood—is the widely known prefix of Mr. S. H. Till, famous as the breeder of the lovely bitch Ch. " Roundwood Lass ". Born in 1932, " Lass " was descended from Ch. " Rufton Recorder " on her sire's side and from Ch. " Hemlington Kalgar " on her dam's side. I remember her as one of our most lovely bitches. By 1935, in which year she won, I think, at least five C.Cs., right on into 1938, where at six years of age she was still defying competition. . . in all she won at least twenty-seven C.Cs. " Roundwood Remember ", a very nice dog, followed on the tradition of this kennel. He was great grandfather to my little " Bramhope Suzette " the dam of " Boxer ". What memories these names revive as I delve into the histories of these dogs of long ago! Nowadays the ' Roundwood ' prefix rarely appears in the show catalogues, but both Mr. and Mrs. Till are well known as championship show judges of the breed.

Rufton—owned by Mr. R. Cornthwaite, whose name goes down in Springer history for that great dog Ch. " Rufton Recorder ", a great influence on the breed both in Britain and in Canada and the U.S.A., where many present-day Champions are descended from him." Ringmaster " was another good one who appeared in the later 1930's just before the Second World War put an end to so many breeding programmes.

of Solway—another long established suffix is that of Mr. R. Grierson, who bred and sold so many good ones in the 1930's. In fact in 1930 alone Mr. Grierson won no less than fourteen C.Cs. with such famous dogs and bitches as Ch. " Advert of Solway ", Ch. " Admiration of Solway ", Ch. " Follow Through of Solway " and Ch. " Lovebird of Solway ". In 1935 Ch. " Winning Number of Solway " was at the peak of his winning, while in

1938 "Queen Mona of Solway" was starting her winning career.

Tedwyns—owned by Mr. A. Byrne, a famous name in Field Trial circles in the 1930's. "Tedwyns Togs", "Trick", "Tailfly" and F.T. Ch. "Tedwyns Trex" were just a few of his many winners.

Timperley—was the prefix used by Mr. R. J. Shoesmith. Dogs from this kennel did some nice winning in the 1930's, "Timperley Topper", "Gun Master", and "Beauty" were probably his best known dogs.

O'Vara—this suffix represented the fine kennel owned by Mr. Selwyn C. Jones of North Wales (also well known in Irish Water Spaniel spheres), a great name in the Field Trial world, closely linked in my mind with that of another, the 'Corndean' prefix owned by Mr. T. J. Greatorex, who handled Mr. Jones' dogs at Field Trials, and always managed to make difficult jobs appear so easy! All through the 1930's the 'O'Vara' reputation went from strength to strength with "Trout O'Vara", "Slick", "Slip", "Stream", "Style" and many others too numerous to list. After the Second World War, the 'O'Vara' stock went to the top again; and since the recent death of Mr. Jones, this affix still lives on in the capable hands of Mr. Greatorex.

of Ware—is, of course, the suffix known (and protected) all over the world and used by Mr. H. S. Lloyd of Middlesex. Nowadays when one thinks of the 'Wizard of Ware' it is his oustanding reputation with Cocker Spaniels that springs first to the mind, and so some of the newcomers to the Springer ranks may not know that, in the 1920's Mr. Lloyd owned many famous English Springers, among them Champions "Springbok of Ware ", " Jambok ", and " Jamson of Ware ". His strain had a great influence on the breed in the U.S.A., where he sent Ch. " Springbok of Ware " and other dogs. Mr. Chevrier who founded the ' Avondale ' kennels in the U.S.A. (not to be confused with our ' Avendale ') imported both " Springbok " and Dual Ch. " Flint of Avendale ".

Mr. Lloyd has always shown intense interest in English Springers long after he ceased to exhibit them, and has always been active on the committee of the English Springer Spaniel Club, and indeed made an excellent chairman for several years. He is in great demand as a judge of the breed here and overseas both at shows and Field Trials, and his criticism is something to be valued. For many years he refused to judge, and I shall always be proud to think that I finally persuaded him to judge Springers at the championship show of the Midland English Springer Spaniel Society in 1953, when I was acting as honorary secretary, and he drew the wonderful entry of 204 in the twenty classes. To see him handle a dog in the ring is an education, looking so nonchalant yet getting just that little extra out of his exhibit without stooping to ' top and tail ', he makes it look so easy, yet I know from chats I have had with him of the hours of preparation that have gone into it beforehand—in my section on exhibiting I will tell you of the advice he has so kindly given to me.

It is impossible in the space of one chapter to list every prefix of the between-the-wars period, but I have tried to recall those best known to most of us.

The years 1938 and 1939 seemed to reflect the unsettled and apprehensive feeling prevalent at that time, and I always think of it as a period of transition between peace and war. Still the shows went on, and we had the

' Canfordborne ' prefix of Mr. J. Roster Latham appearing in the limelight with Ch. "Canfordborne Mediant ", " Vivace ", and " Dream Girl ". Miss O. Strickland of Preston (who still makes the occasional appearance in the show ring today) was winning with her ' Art ' dogs, " Artist's Model ", " Specialist " and others.

Mrs. F. Travers was winning well with her grand dog " Totonian Finder " and his litter brother " Sportsman of Toton ". Mrs. Travers was a great supporter of the breed when shows recommenced in 1943, and she and her husband were enthusiastic joint secretaries of the English Springer Spaniel Club for several years. I am sorry that they have given up their active interest in the breed lately.

Then we had the late Mrs. Gertrude Thomson with her "Invincible George " and " Hopeful Judy ". Her prefix of ' Cliftonhouse ' became well known, and although she saw her " Clintonhouse Hazeltong Judith " (now mine, and still going strong although nearly twelve years old) winning her C.Cs., she never lived to see "Judith"s son Ch. " Clintonhouse George " gain his title.

In those years Mr. M. D. Withers founded the famous ' Shotton ' kennels at Stratford-on-Avon, where with Mrs. Gwen Broadley at the helm they leapt to fame. Many great dogs came from this kennel: possibly the one with the most influence on the breed being Int. Ch. " Showman of Shotton ", by " Beauchief Outcross " out of " Betty of Highedge ". Mr. Withers also owned Ch. " Jess of Shelcot " and Ch. " Beauchief Barham ". During the war years came " Peter of Shotton ", born at a time when there were no championship shows, but whose influence still shows in the pedigrees of to-day.

Another dog with a great influence on the breed was

Mr. T. Naisby's Ch. "Pleasant Peter", whose son, "Peter's Benefactor" owned by Mr. G. R. Musgrave won over 500 awards in the early 1940's, but owing to the absence of the shows never won his title. It was unfortunate that he died following a wasp sting in the mouth at a fairly early age.

CHAPTER III

CONTEMPORARY DOGS

DURING the Second World War championship shows ceased, but the various canine societies all over Great Britain tried to maintain interest in canine matters with sanction shows and match meetings.

A few breeders carried on limited breeding programmes in spite of feeding difficulties. One of the biggest kennels at this time was that of Mrs. N. Howard of the 'Chastleton' affix, whose lovely bitch " Charming of Chastleton " had won a reserve C.C. just before championship shows ceased. She was a daughter of Ch. " Dry Toast ", and bred many good ones. Mrs. Howard was a great worker for the breed, and her enthusiasm founded the Midland English Springer Spaniel Society— the brilliant first open show of this society held in 1946 and already mentioned, really put the breed in the public eye again.

I still have the press cuttings from this first post-war open show, and it is interesting to recall some of the major awards. Best exhibit in show was Mr. G. A. Taylor's " Carnfield Field Marshall ", while the best bitch was " Staitley Sunlight " owned by the Edinburgh breeder Mr. George Harwell. His stud dog " Staitley Success " was well known; while " Staitley Skymaster " was another good one from this kennel, and, perhaps loveliest of all, his " Staitley May Queen ", bred in Ireland. Of recent years pressure of business has prevented Mr. Harwell from exhibiting, although he can still be seen judging the breed.

Mrs. Olga Hampton, now the popular honorary secretary of the English Springer Spaniel Club (jointly with her husband Ian) was winning with her " Pixie of Larkstoke ", given to them as a wedding present! Mrs. W. Selby-Lowndes (now Lady Angela Lambe) won the maiden dog class with " Whaddon Chase Bonny Tom ", who later became a Champion and sired many big winners.

Miss Morland Hooper, whose 'Ranscombe' kennel had been evacuated from the perils of London to the comparative safety of Windsor to be cared for by her friend Dr. E. Rickards of the 'Tarbay' prefix, won junior dog with " Reveller of Ranscombe ". Mr. Dick Morgan was also there in the awards with " Leymor Binx Bin " who went on to win C.Cs. Miss Dorothy Cupit was there too, with her grand bitch " Sue of Amberside ", and " Ambergris Alert ".

Many pre-war judges were present including Mr. F. Warner Hill, Col. Carrell and Mr. W. East. Their opinions of the exhibits were mixed: Mr. East thought they compared favourably with pre-war dogs, Col. Carrell thought they lacked character, Mr. Warner Hill, said he was disappointed, and the judge Mr. McNab Chassels considered they were not up to pre-war championship show merit . . . such was the start of 1946.

Later, in July, the Midland Society ran another open show at Leeds and drew 230 entries in the twenty-four classes. Mr. East and Mr. J. Gibson judged. Mr. Joe Braddon took the supreme award with " Starshine of

Ide "; this great dog was by " Peter of Shotton " out of Ch. " Jess of Shelcot ".

It was at this show that a party of Irishmen turned up with some good Springers. Mr. Bob Cleland had brought over a brace of youngsters called " Stand Back " and " Come Back ", who were later purchased by Mr. Joe Braddon and Mrs. Gwen Broadley. " Stand Back " became the famous Ch. " Invader of Ide ", who won twenty-five C.Cs. under twenty-five different judges, and whose wins included Best in Show at Brighton when he was eight years old [Joe tells me that he is, at the time of writing, still fit and well]! " Come Back ", later to take Mrs. Broadley's prefix became " Sandylands Starling ", and was winning well, but unfortunately was killed in the terrible fire at Sandy Lands in 1947, when the kennels were destroyed and several valuable dogs lost their lives.

Mrs. Broadley's " Sandylands Showgirl " was a cup winner at this Leeds show. Miss D. Cupit's " Ambergris Harvester " was best bitch. My " Boxer of Bramhope ", who had won the puppy cup at the first open show at Derby repeated the performance at Leeds. A new prefix emerged too at Leeds, that of ' Happeedaze ' owned by Mr. W. Rankin Hepplewhite, who won with " Start ", and also with " Sprightly of Happeedaze " who in due course became a Champion.

Later in 1946 the breed societies held championship shows. The English Springer Spaniel Club held its show at Reading, with Mr. Ernest Trimble as judge; then the Midland Society with Mr. W. Humphrey judging; and in November the English Springer Spaniel Club of Northern Ireland with Mrs. Gwen Broadley as judge. C.Cs. were won by Mr. G. A. Taylor and Mr. S. Holmes with " Carnfield Christabelle ", Mr. R. A. Morgan's

" Leymor Binx Bin ", Mrs. Gwen Broadley's " Sandy-lands Sherry ", Mr. J. Braddon's " Starshine of Ide ", and Lady A. Lambe's " Whaddon Chase Bonny Tom ".

In 1947 the first post-war all-breed championship show was held at Peterborough, with " Whaddon Chase Bonny Tom " and " Sandylands Showgirl " winning the C.Cs. in English Springers. The ' Sandylands ' kennel was ' tops ' in 1947, winning nine C.Cs. with " Sherry ", " Shot ", " Showgirl " and " Shrubly ". Joe Braddon's ' Ide ' kennel was close behind with six C.Cs. with " Invader " (previously " Stand Back ") and "Star-shine", and Lady Lambe was level with six C.Cs. with "Bonny Tom ", Ch. " Whaddon Chase Snipe ", " Whad-don Chase Titch " and " Higham Tristram ".

This then was the picture before us as the stage was set and the curtain rolled up on the next ten years of English Springer history! Here I would like to pay tribute to one of the immortals of the U.S.A., the American and Canadian Champion " Frejax Royal Salute ", owned by the late Mr. Fred Jackson who was born in Manchester, and who served in the Royal Flying Corps in First World War). " Royal Salute " was born in 1945, and had thirty-one Best in Show victories in the U.S.A. and seven in Canada. He also won fifty-five sporting groups in the U.S.A. and eleven in Canada. He sired twenty-six Champions in-cluding the great Am. Ch. " Melilotus Royal Oak ", owned by my very dear friend Mrs. R. Gilman Smith; " Oak " was proclaimed ' Sire of the Year ' at the National Show of 1958.

In 1948, honours were more evenly divided, and new names began creeping to the top—Mr. W. Rankin Hepplewhite scored the highest number of C.G.s with Ch. " Solitaire of Happeedaze " and " Sprightly of

Happeedaze " who won three each that year. " Solitaire " was bred in Ireland by Mr. E. V. Power, and was by " Peter of Shotton " out of " Drumcree Joan ". Mr. G. A. Taylor was close with four C.Cs. with " Carnfield Albvic Legioner ", later to become a Champion, " Carnfield Chick", and " Carnfield Field Marshall "; close too was Mrs. Broadley with " Sandylands Shot ", and " Sandylands Shrubly " who now claimed the proud title of Champion. Mr. G. Harwell won four C.Cs. with his Ch. " Staitley May Queen ", and Lady Lambe kept in the lead with " Whaddon Chase Bracken ", Ch. " Whaddon Chase Snipe ", and the black and white bitch, purchased from Mr. Naisby, " Claxton Outspan ". Mr. W. R. Johnston's lovely bitch " Whintonhill Tessa ", home bred by " Northern Command " out of " Beautility Brocade ", won four C.Cs. in 1948, and was later bought by Mr. A. B. Nicolson, whose ' Glenbervie ' prefix had been in the limelight in Cockers all through the 1930's, and who was now to head the lists among English Springer breeders for many years.

Mr. D. C. Hannah, who has now been the popular chairman of the Midland Society for many years, won three C.Cs. in 1948 with his Ch. " Stokeley Bonny Boy ". " Bonny Boy " was sired by Lady Lambe's Ch. " Whaddon Chase Bonny Tom ", out of " Clintonhouse Elizabeth ". Mr. Joe Braddon's Ch. " Invader of Ide " kept up his run with three C.Cs. in 1948, and two new names crept into the C.C. list in " Boxer of Bramhope " and his son " Grand Lodge ", owned by Mr. R. Cleland, who later won eleven C.Cs. but who unfortunately died quite young.

During the war years Ireland had been able to keep up a better breeding programme than the other countries of the British Isles, and consequently quite a lot of winners were appearing from over the water. Mr. W. R. Gardiner's "Cavehill Maid", and Mr. F. J. Burton's lovely bitch Ch. "Painted Lady" were two who I remember very well. Mr. E. Lumb Taylor purchased "Sandylands Soubranie" from Mrs. Broadley and won two C.Cs. in 1948 with him. This dog was later to sire the well-known dog of to-day, Mrs. Joan Midgley's Ch. "Mowgrain Mr. Chips". And also in 1948 Mr. and Mrs. S. H. Till won one C.C. with "Roundwood Roger the Rake", as did Mrs. F. Travers with "Totonian Belle".

The year 1949 was "Grand Lodge"'s year, when he headed the dog C.C. list with six, followed by Ch. "Invader of Ide" with four; the Irish-bred "Cavehill Maid" led the bitch list with five C.Cs., and "Whinton-hill Tessa", Mr. G. A. Taylor's "Carnfield Florrie" and Miss Francis' "Higham Topsy" (who won her title) all won three C.Cs. Lady Lambe won three with "Whaddon Chase Prince" and "Whaddon Chase Bracken", both of whom became Champions later on. Mrs. Broadley took two with Ch. "Sandylands Shrubly" and "Sandylands Shandy", with "Soubranie" gaining another C.C. for Mr. E. Lumb Taylor. Mr. D. C. Hannah brought out a brother of "Bonny Boy" in "Stokeley Gay Boy" to win his first C.C. Still more new names came into the ranks of C.C. winners when Mr. E. W. Dudgon won his first with "Jess of Montcrief", by "Chastleton Waxwing", who later became a Champion. Mr. I. ('Sandy') Davies from Pinxton won two tickets with "Colmaris Toreador", and Major A. M. Horsbrugh, although more interested in the Field Trial side of the game, won two C.Cs. with his dog "Strathblane Bonnie". The 'Winch' prefix of

Mr. G. G. Crawford appeared among the tickets in 1949 when he won with his " Winch Agate ".

From Newcastle-on-Tyne, Mr. F. L. Davy sent a bitch called " Alwinton Faithful Maid " to be mated to " Boxer ", and the resulting litter were brought up the hard way, in an upstairs flat on the edge of the Town Moor. All credit must go to Mr. Davy on his rearing, for out of this litter came two future Champions, the first, " Light of Ashleigh ", was bought by Mr. A. B. Nicolson and won her first C.C. in 1949, then going on to win fourteen C.Cs. and the supreme honour of Best in Show at Manchester ch. show in 1951. The other was bought as a pet for his little girl, Hilary, by Mr. Jimmy Hanning of Newcastle and was unshown for a couple of years, being almost three years old before he won his first C.C. You probably remember this great dog became Ch. " Peter of Lorton Fell ", winning twelve C.Cs. in all, Best in Show at Ayr ch. show in 1953, Best in Show two years running at the English Springer Spaniel Club's breed ch. shows, and winner of the Gundog Groups at the L.K.A. and W.E.L.K.S. championship shows.

In 1950 Mrs. Broadley brought out a new one to become a Champion, " Castlecary Cameronian ". Bred in Scotland as the name implies, he won three C.Cs. in a row for his new owner, and was sold to the U.S.A. Mrs. Broadley's " Sandylands Shandy " also won three C.Cs. that year. Lady Lambe's " Whaddon Chase Prince " became a Champion and won four C.Cs. and her " Primula " won her first. Mr. R. A. Morgan won two C.Cs. with " Leymor Recorder ", who later became a Champion. Miss D. Cupit won two, with " Ambergris Alert ", as did Mrs. Travers with " Totonian Biddy ", but little by little new names and new faces were arriving.

From Scotland came Mr. J. Bolton with the lovely bitch " Tillan Toddy " to win the first of her fifteen C.Cs., fourteen of them under different judges. Also from Scotland came Mr. G. H. Smellie's " Millheugh Dainty Maid " to win a C.C., while over from Ireland Mr. H. Hunt's " My Love of Bournview " won two C.Cs. that year. Dr. Aubrey Ireland won two C.Cs. with " Birkdale Beggarmaid ", handled by Mr. R. A. Morgan. Mrs. N. Howard won one with " Jet of Chastleton ", and Mr. E. Froggatt won his first ever with his black-and-white dog " Bramhope Recorder ", who was by the Irish black-and-white dog "Ideal Stamp" out of "Bramhope Suzette". "Recorder" later became a Champion. Mr. G. R. Musgrave of " Peter's Benefactor " fame, won his first C.C. with " Dinsdale Dame ", and his neighbour Mr. W. Rankin Hepplewhite won one with " Simon of Happeedaze ".

More new names crept into the ranks of Challenge Certificate winning exhibitors in the year 1951. Miss Joan Wilkins (now Mrs. Tom Dinwoodie) won three C.Cs. with a son of " Grand Lodge " called " Banner of Beechfield ". This grand young dog was bred by Mrs. Frank Thompson, whose husband was chairman of the Midland Society for several years. This dog was out of the lovely bitch " Bountiful of Beechfield ", who later joined the ' Studley ' kennel of Mr. and Mrs. S. G. Smithson, and won one C.C. for them.

My sister, Miss Betty Cripps, also won three with a son of " Boxer ", " Banker of Bramhope ". Lady Lambe kept level with Ch. " Whaddon Chase Prince ", as did Mrs. Broadley with Ch. " Sandylands Shandy " while " Peter of Lorton Fell " won his first two C.Cs. that year.

Close on the heels of these four dogs, came "Alexander of Stubham ", to win his first two C.Cs. that year, owned by Mrs. F. O. Till of Ilkley. The ' Stubham ' exhibits had been knocking at the door with several good ones sired by " Boxer " out of their foundation bitch " Susan of Stubham ", bred by Mrs. A. T. Sowter of Addingham. Later " Alex " went on to great glory, winning twenty-two C.Cs. under twenty-one different judges, and became one of our best-known Champions.

From Wales came Mr. R. G. Thomas with " Skipper of Happeedaze " to win two Certificates, and Mr. D. C. Hannah brought out another good dog in " Stokeley Lucky ", who later became a Champion. Honours in bitches went to Scotland, with Mr. J. Bolton's " Tillan Toddy " in the lead with four C.Cs. in 1951. Mr. A. B. Nicolson won two with " Deana of Glenbervie " and " Light of Ashleigh ". Mrs. O. M. C. Hampton won her ' first ever ' with " Larkstoke Skylark ", and Lady Lambe won two with " Whaddon Chase Bonny Lass ", while the remaining honours went to the winning bitches of 1950 already mentioned.

By 1952, Chs. " Alexander of Stubham " and " Invader of Ware " were neck and neck with four C.Cs. each in the year, while Ch. " Stokeley Lucky " chalked up another three. Then into the picture came Mr. I. Davies with " Clintonhouse George " to win three C.Cs. in the year—and his title. Two new ticket winners were Mr. E. A. Anderson with " Bracken of Crosslane ", and Miss Prudence Austin with " Burleeds Brigadier of Bramhope ". In bitches " Tillan Toddy " reigned supreme winning eight more C.Cs., leaving just a few for Mr. and

Plate V

Maud Earl's beautiful painting of " Tissington Flush ".

Canis Dog Features.

Two Norfolks from Shaw's
Illustrated Book of the Dog, 1879-80.

Canis Dog Features.

B. Smith's engraving after a painting by Stubbs.

Canis Dog Features.

Plate VI

F. Winton Smith's Ch.
" Beachgrove
        Donaldson ",
    about 1905.

H. S. Lloyd's Ch.
" Springbok of Ware "

Photo by Hedges.

The bitch Ch.
" Inveresk
Coronation ",
born 1923.

Mrs. S. H. Till's "Roundwood Haynford Lady", Mr. G. A. Taylor's Ch. "Carnfield Chick" and "Carnfield Christabelle" owned by Mrs. R. Dawson, Mrs. F. O. Till's "Sheila of Stubham", Mrs. D. Beal's "Amanda of Stubham", Mrs. N. Howard's "Chastleton Lucky Lady", and Lady Lambe's "Whaddon Chase Romance" and "Whaddon Chase Swift".

The following year, 1953, saw little change of scene for Ch. "Invader" still led the field winning six C.Cs. in the following year, followed closely by Ch. "Alexander" and Ch. "Clintonhouse George" with five each. But coming to the top came a new force, Mrs. S. M. Smithson's "Studley Major" winning three C.Cs. that year, and later winning his title. Both Ch. "Stokeley Gay Boy" and Ch. "Peter of Lorton Fell" won two more while Mr. E. Froggatt's "Bramhope Recorder" scored another. From Scarborough came Mrs. V. Hare-Dinsley to win her first with "Camdin Chief" (by "Boxer" out of "Camdin Mistress Lucy"). "Chief" later won his title. Many new bitches came to the fore in 1953.

From Scotland Mr. Nicolson won three C.Cs. with "Wollburn Wallflower", bred by Mrs. H. Bell from her "Wollburn Wattie Honey". From the North, Mr. Rod Grant won three tickets with his "Dinah of Stubham" (bred by Mrs. F. O. Till from "Susan" by "Boxer") who later won her title. Mr. I. Davies brought out a new home-bred bitch in "Colmaris Contessa", by "Colmaris Toreador" out of "Clintonhouse Hazeltong Judith".

Lady Lambe had a good run with "Whaddon Chase Grouse","Romance" and "Swift", while Mrs. Travers won with "Totonian Comet", and Mr. Musgrave with "Dinsdale Donna". Mr. Parks from Ireland was successful with " Linwhinny Ladybird ", Mr. E. A. Anderson scored with " Candida of Crosslane ", and my " Belarosa of Bramhope " began her winning career by winning two C.Cs. that year.

A great year for Mr. I. Davies was 1954, for in that year his Ch. " Clintonhouse George " won no less than nine C.Cs. Chs. " Alexander of Stubham " and " Peter of Lorton Fell " were level with four tickets each in the year, and only three new names broke into this winning circle. These were Mr. W. Black from Ireland with " Rugby Lad " who won one C.C. that year; Mrs. S. M. Smithson with " Studley Brave Buccaneer " who won his first; " Buccaneer " was by " Boxer " out of that great bitch " Bountiful of Beechfield ", as was the American Champion " Studley Hercules"; and Mr. D. Campbell from Scotland who won with his " Inverruel Raider ", who later became a Champion.

Yes, 1954, was truly a year to remember for ' Sandy ' Davies, for his Ch. " Colmaris Contessa " led the field in bitches with six C.Cs. that year! Ch. " Belarosa of Bramhope " followed on with three, and in to the ranks came Mr. Harold Frankish from Scarborough, piloting his wife's " Beanmore Camdin Greta " to win three Certificates and to become a Champion.

Mr. Nicolson brought out a new ticket winner in " Princess of Glenbervie ", as did Mrs. F. Oughtred Till with " Hazel of Stubham ". Mr. H. Evans, a newcomer from Wirral went to the top with his " Bramble Amber ", and in Ireland " Pride of Abbotscross " won at the Belfast Championship Show.

It must have been a terrible blow to Mr. Davies to lose Ch. " Clintonhouse George " at an early age, and all the English Springer world mourned his loss.

Ch. "Alexander of Stubham" took the lead in 1955 winning six C.Cs. followed by "Studley Brave Buccaneer" with four, Ch. "Peter of Lorton Fell" with two, and "Camdin Chief" winning three in a row at Blackpool, Windsor, and Paignton. Mr. Nicolson brought out "Mallard of Glenbervie" to win his first C.C., and my "Beagle of Bramhope" scored one. From Ireland came Mr. R. Burton to win his first with "Print of Ardrick". This lovely dog became an International Champion, home-bred by Ch. "Clintonhouse George". I was proud to give him Best of Breed at Cruft's in 1958, and his owner's sudden death not long after came as a great shock to us all. Lt.-Col. L. H. Morris, now well known in Labrador circles, won his first C.C. with "Artistry Raffles" in 1955. But by the Christmas of 1955 another great English Springer was lost to the breed, when Mr. J. C. Hanning's Ch. "Peter of Lorton Fell" died after a short illness.

Also during 1955 Ch. "Belarosa of Bramhope" led the way in bitches with five tickets in the year, followed by "Wollburn Wallflower" and "Hazel of Stubham" with three each, while "Bathsheba of Bramhope" scored her first two. "Jessica of Stubham" scored two for Mr. Glyn Lewis of Machynlleth, Wales, as did Ch. "Colmaris Contessa" for 'Sandy' Davies. Lady Lambe had one with "Whaddon Chase Salote", while Miss Francis took one with Ch. "Higham Topsy". Down in Paignton Mr. and Mrs. S. Reast won their very first C.C. with their "Foxglove of Stubham", Mrs. T. Spence of London won one with "Brandyhole Bellflower".

Mr. D. C. Hannah took the lead in 1956 with a son of Ch. "Clintonhouse George" called "Stokeley Sea Sprite", who won five C.Cs. in the year, his litter sister, "Stokeley Sea Princess" also doing well and winning

two that year—their dam was "Stokeley Flight".
Honours were fairly evenly divided in 1956 really,
" Inverruel Raider " scored two tickets, " Print of Ardrick " two, Mr. R. G. Thomas' " Conquest of Clyne "
from Wales scored two, and after a run of several re-
serves, Mr. E. E. A. Stevenson's " Bonaventure of
Bramhope " scored two.

"Bonaventure of Bramhope" was bred by Mrs. A. T.
Sowter, of the ' Stonebrig ' prefix, out of her " Stonebrig
Seraph " by " Boxer "; thus he is litter brother to my
" Beagle ".

After these came Ch. " Alexander of Stubham " and
his son " Royal Salute of Stubham ", with one each,
the younger dog later becoming a Champion, but
dying young from the after effects of Rubarth's disease,
from which he had made a wonderful recovery as a
puppy, only to become paralysed just as he had attained
maturity. Mrs. Smithson won a C.C. each with Ch.
" Studley Major ", and " Studley Brave Buccaneer ";
Mr. A. B. Nicolson one with " Mallard of Glenbervie ",
and Miss C. M. Francis one with " Higham Barney
Blazer "; while " Burleeds Brigadier of Bramhope "
scored one.

Mr. and Mrs. T. Dinwoodie brought out a new son
of " Banker " called " Lochar Smokey ", to win his
first C.C., and a new star emerged in " Mowgrain Mr.
Chips ", bred by Mrs. Joan Midgley of Bacup in Lancashire. By " Sandylands Soubranie " out of " Bambino of
Bramhope ", " Mr. Chips " won his first C.C. at Belfast under Mr. F. Parsons, the author of the forthcoming *Labrador Retriever Handbook* in this series.

Mrs. Midgley, a busy district nurse, had to take " Mr.
Chips " as a wee pup around with her (not in her little
black bag but in the back of her car) while she did her

rounds, and bottle-fed him between visits. However, her care was amply repaid as he went on to become a Champion winning a goodly number of C.Cs.; even so much credit must also go to Mr. G. Mason who piloted him to win his first C.C. and to Mr. E. Cudworth who handled him to win many more. Another son of Ch. " Clintonhouse George ", " Beauvallet of Crosslane ", bred and owned by Mr. Anderson, won the C.C. at the L.K.A. championship show that year.

Many good bitches appeared in that year of 1956: Ch. " Belarosa of Bramhope " led with three C.Cs., and " Bathsheba of Bramhope " scored her third which made her a Champion. Mr. J. S. Webster's " Bonnie Wee Teal " scored two more, as did Mr. Glyn Lewis' " Jessica of Stubham ".

Also from Wales came Mr. J. Williams' " Mably Sharon " to win two tickets. The litter sister to " Print of Ardrick ", called " Prim of Ardrick ", won for Mr. F. J. Burton; and Mrs. T. Spence from London scored two with " Duchess of Stubham "—bred by Mrs. Oughtred Till. This bitch later won her title. Another daughter of " Boxer ", " Bowbell of Bramhope ", owned by Mr. J. Evans of Hereford, won her first C.C., as did Mrs. M. Woods from Cheshire with her " Woodsorrel Jenny Wren ", and Mr. S. Dooley from Derbyshire with his " Colmaris Tawny Jewel ".

" Stokeley Sea Princess " chalked up another two, Lady Lambe scored one with " Whaddon Chase Salote ", Mrs. Smithson one with " Studley Annabelle ", and Mrs. O. Hampton with " Larkstoke Sugarcandy ".

Although competition was keen the year 1957 made Mrs. Midgley's Ch. " Mowgrain Mr. Chips " the star dog with a total of five C.Cs. in the year. Honours were fairly evenly divided among the dogs, with Ch. " Royal

Salute of Stubham ", " Beauvallet of Crosslane ", " Bona-venture of Bramhope ", " Studley Brave Buccaneer ", and Int. Ch. " Print of Ardrick " all scoring two Certifi-cates each, while Ch. " Inverruel Raider " and " Lochar Smokey ", both from Scotland, scored one each. Mrs. H. P. Frankish from Scarborough brought out a smart young dog in " Colmaris Chancellor ", bred by Mr. Davies, to win the C.C. at Richmond.

From the Scottish Borders Mrs. R. Clark won one C.C. with " Dryburgh Thistle ", Mr. Hannah scored one with a new youngster, " Stokeley Falcon ", and my old friend from Carlisle, Mr. W. R. Johnston (who bred " Whintonhill Tessa " and many good ones in the past), brought out his " Whintonhill Raider " to win his first C.C. at Birmingham. Mr. E. E. A. Stevenson from Col-chester took the ticket at Hove with his young dog " Castlelea Squadronaire ", his first.

In bitches, Mr. Hannah's " Stokeley Sea Princess " had a brilliant 1957 winning five C.Cs. in the year. Mrs. F. Sherwood and Mr. M. Manin's tri-colour " Northdown Donna " came next with three, and Miss Judith M. Robinson's " Onyx of Stubham " scored two. Mrs. H. Patey, a newcomer to the Springer ranks although she had shown Cockers for a number of years, won two C.Cs. with her "Brown Bess of Bramhope ", purchased from me, and bred by Mrs. Smithson of the ' Studley ' prefix.

Other well-known winning bitches had to be content with one C.C. each in the year: Ch. " Bonnie Wee Teal ", Ch. " Colmaris Contessa ", " Brandyhole Berry Brown ", " Studley Diadem ", " Pride of Abbots-cross ", "Duchess of Stubham ", Lady Lambe's " Whad-don Chase Salote " and " Whaddon Chase Destiny ". From Scotland Mr. I. E. Lynch won one C.C. with

" Duskie Princess ", and from the South Mrs. M. L. Diamond won one with " Julia of Hatherley ".

As I write this in the snow and fog of January 1959, the last year is but a very recent memory, a pleasantly exciting year with honours rather more evenly divided than in previous years. In dogs, Ch. "Mowgrain Mr. Chips " just held his lead again with another five C.Cs., but Mr. Stevenson's "Bonaventure of Bramhope " was close up with four C.Cs. Mr. Davies brought out a smart youngster " Colmaris Nice Fella " and won four tickets with him, thus still furthering the fame of the ' Colmaris ' prefix; while running close Mrs. Frankish's Ch. " Colmaris Chancellor " chalked up a further three.

Mrs. Oughtred Till also brought out a new youngster called " Studley Grenadier of Stubham ". Bred by Mrs. Smithson, he won two C.Cs. and has since won his qualifying Certificate at Field Trials. Up at Ayr, Mr. Nicolson brought his " Mallard of Glenbervie " out of retirement to win one C.C., and at Cruft's Int. Ch. " Print of Ardrick " won his last before the tragic death of his owner—since when we have not seen this grand dog in the show ring up to the time of writing.

Towards the end of the year two happy people won their very first C.Cs.: Mr. J. J. Parnell with his " Studley Dragoon ", another grand dog from Mrs. Smithson's kennel, and Miss J. Manifold with her " Dovehouse Wonder Boy ", bred by that enthusiastic exhibitor, Mrs. Berta Lancashire, who had been trying for a number of years to achieve her ambition to win a C.C., and who was naturally quite thrilled by Miss Manifold's win.

Mrs. Sherwood had a great year with her nice black-and-white bitch, " Vanity Fair of Stubham ", bred by Mrs. Oughtred Till, when she won four C.Cs., as did Mrs. Till's " Studley Diadem ". Mrs. Campbell Durie brought out a young daughter of her "Brandyhole Berry Brown " carrying her own suffix ' of Kilduskland ', and called " Eriska of Kilduskland ". This bitch won two C.Cs., while her dam had to be content with just one more in the year. Mrs. Till brought out a new young bitch " Sheila of Stubham " to win two C.Cs. and Miss Judith Robinson scored two more with her " Onyx of Stubham". My six-year-old Ch. " Belarosa of Bramhope " won two Certificates and her kennel companion Ch. " Bathsheba of Bramhope " scored one, but was proud to see her daughter " Barnadine of Bramhope " score her first two C.Cs. Ch. "Northdown Donna ", " Brown Bess of Bramhope " and " Duskie Princess " also scored one each. Indeed competition in bitches during 1958 was particularly strong, and no new faces appeared in the list of Challenge Certificate winners.

You will notice that I have only mentioned the lucky exhibitors who have won Certificates in this post-war period, for in a single chapter it would be physically impossible to mention *all* the many promising dogs and their owners who have won minor honours through the years—the section would become a mere catalogue of names. However, so many good ones are knocking at the door of fame, and may yet receive the big green cards that I simply must mention just a few of the 1958 exhibitors whose dogs I can recall and to whom I would like to say ' keep on knocking ': Mrs. H. M. S. Bell of the ' Wollburn ' prefix; Mrs. R. Campion from Beckenham; Miss Helen Cooper of Shipley; those grand supporters of the breed, the 'Winch ' Crawford's; Mr. F. Dawson and Mrs. G. A. and Mrs. M. M. Johnson of Sheffield; Miss Gillian Dewhirst; Mrs. G. Dobson from Darlington; Mr. G. R. Scott; Mr. W. Findlay from Scotland; Mrs. D. L. George from Hampshire; Mrs.

G. B. Hartley from Lancs.; Mr. G. Jones from Clitheroe and Mr. K. Jones from Cheshire; Mr. J. Malarkey from Stockport; Mr. G. Mason from Preston; Mr. Victor Midgley, stepson of Mrs. Joan Midgley; the Muirhead family from Cromer; Mr. C. F. Stephenson from Market Harborough; Mr. A. G. Warnes from Leicester; Mr. E. Wearne from Devon; Dr. W. G. P. Wells of Chesterfield; Miss M. E. Wilkins from Shropshire; Mr. D. J. Williams from London, that grand worker for the breed; Mrs. Maureen Williams of Aberystwyth; Mr. E. C. Woodham from Herts.; and Mrs. M. Wright from Liverpool. And I must not overlook Mrs. Mollie Edwards, my good friend from Hollingworth; Mr. Arthur Froggatt, father of Ernest Froggatt; Mrs. H. Fussey from Bridlington; Mrs. A. C. Hodgkin from Leicester; Mrs. Anna Redlich the author, and the Springer folk over the water in Ireland; Mrs. D. M. Senior from Sheffield; Mr. and Mrs. F. Waterhouse of Scarborough; and Mrs. D. Watkinson from Lincolnshire.

CHAPTER IV

The Standard

The general appearance of the modern English Springer Spaniel is that of a symmetrical, compact, strong, upstanding, merry and active dog, built for endurance and activity. He is the highest on the leg and raciest of build of all land Spaniels.

Head—The skull should be of medium length and fairly broad and slightly rounded, rising from the foreface, making a brow or stop, divided by a fluting between the eyes gradually dying away along the forehead towards the occiput bone, which should not be peaked. The cheeks should be flat, that is, not rounded or full. The foreface should be of proportionate length to the skull, fairly broad and deep without being coarse, well chiselled below the eyes, fairly deep and square in flew, but not exaggerated to such an extent as would interfere with comfort when retrieving. Nostrils well developed, underjaw strong and level mouth, that is neither over- nor under-shot.

Eye—The eye should be neither too full nor too small, but of medium size, not prominent nor sunken but well set in (not showing haw), of an alert, kindly expression. A mouse-like eye without expression is objectionable; as also is a light eye. The colour should be dark hazel.

Ears—The ears should be lobular in shape, set close to the head, of good length and width, but not exaggerated. The correct set should be in a line with the eye.

Neck—The neck should be strong and muscular, of nice length and free from throatiness, well set in the shoulders, nicely arched and tapering towards the head—this giving great activity and speed. A ewe neck is objectionable.

Body—The body should be strong and of proportionate length, neither too long nor too short, the chest deep and well developed with plenty of heart and lung room, well sprung ribs, loins muscular and strong with slight arch and well coupled, thighs broad and muscular and well developed.

Stern—The stern should be low and never carried above the level of the back, well feathered and with a lively action.

Forelegs—The forelegs should be straight and nicely feathered, elbows set well to body and with proportionate substance to carry the body, strong flexible pasterns, feet tight, compact and well rounded with strong full pads.

Hind Legs–The hind legs should be well let down from hip to hocks. Stifles and hocks moderately bent, inclining neither inwards nor outwards. Coarseness of hocks objectionable.

Movement—The English Springer gait is strictly his own. His forelegs should swing straight forward from the shoulder, throwing the feet well forward in an easy and free manner, not a paddle nor choppy Terrier-like stride. His hocks should drive well under his body, following in a line with his forelegs. At slow movement many English Springers have a pacing stride typical of the breed.

Coat—The coat should be close, straight and weather resisting without being coarse.

Colour—Any recognized land Spaniel colour is acceptable, but liver-and-white, black-and-white, or either of these colours with tan markings, preferred.

Height—The approximate height should be 20 in.

Weight—The approximate weight should be 50 lb.

Scale of Points

Head and Jaws	10
Eyes	5
Ears	5
Neck	10
Body	20
Forelegs	10
Hind legs	10
Feet	10
Stern	10
Coat and Feather	10
Total Positive Points ...	100

The above is the revised Standard of Points as approved by the English Springer Spaniel Club of England, the English Springer Spaniel Club of Scotland, and the Spaniel Club of Scotland, on the 16th May, 1934.

It may well be that after this period of a quarter of a century, the various breed clubs would do well to get together and perhaps clarify the Standard and bring it more up to date. Our American friends have already done this, and in 1956 a greatly lengthened, precise, well worded breed Standard was approved by the American Kennel Club. One of the important omissions in our Standard is that of *Temperament*, and I now quote from the American Standard:

> The typical Springer is friendly, eager to please, quick to learn, willing to obey. In the show ring he should exhibit poise, attentiveness and tractability, and should permit himself to be examined by the judge without resentment or cringing.
>
> *To be penalized*—Excessive timidity, with due allowance for puppies and novice exhibits. But no dog to receive a ribbon if he behaves in vicious manner towards handler or judge. Aggressiveness towards other dogs in the ring not to be construed as viciousness.

I quote now a few of the further points which are penalized in the American Standard, and which I think are such serious faults that I would like to see our British Standard make mention of them.

> *Eyes*—Eyes yellow or brassy in colour, sharp expression indicating unfriendly or suspicious nature. Loose droopy lids.
>
> *Neck*—Short neck, often the sequence to steep shoulders.

Body—Body too shallow indicating lack of brisket. Ribs too flat sometimes due to immaturity. Ribs too round (barrel shaped) hampering the gait. Sway back and roach back.

Tail—Tail habitually upright. Tail set too high or too low. Clamped down tail (indicating timidity or undependable temperament even less to be desired than the tail carried too gaily).

You will see by the above that our American friends are realizing the importance of a good temperament in the breed—so many bad faults go with bad temperaments. I will list just a few: A hard, brassy eye, and sharp expression goes with bad temper; gay tail with aggressiveness; cringing with a sly, suspicious nature; heavy, wet, slobbery lips with nervousness.

Of all the points mentioned in the Standard, *Size* has caused the most controversy, the word 'approximate' being interpreted as 'close to' or 'nearly'; but how near, or how close to the 20 in. named in the Standard are we to try to aim? Is an inch each way too much to allow? A dog must be masculine, and I think I am safe in stating that most of our dog Champions would measure 21 in. or thereabouts, some even more.

But general balance must be taken into consideration, and a big dog, correctly balanced, with good depth of brisket can cause an optical illusion, and appear the same size as a smaller dog with shallow brisket. This can give the appearance of being higher on the leg. To emphasise femininity a bitch should naturally be smaller than her male counterpart, and here possibly 19 in. to 20 in. is the ideal. Height is taken from the set on of the shoulder-blades to the ground, I use a flat yardstick with a sliding set square to rest on the shoulder, and this seems fairly accurate, it is interesting to measure the growth of puppies in this way.

Fantastic stories have always been told of the height and weight of some of our famous winners, it has often been said that Triple Int. Ch. " Showman of Shotton ", from whom many of our present-day winners are descended, was a big dog measuring 22 in. When he was in America, that great American authority on the English Springer, Mr. Maxwell Riddle, devised special equipment for measuring them, and he states emphatically that the height of " Showman " was 20 in! With the same apparatus he measured that great American sire Int. Ch. " Frejax Royal Salute ", and his height was $20\frac{1}{2}$ in. My own " Boxer of Bramhope " was often referred to in the ring as a 'little' dog (doubtless his heavy bone and deep brisket gave that impression), yet I measured him many times and he was just $\frac{1}{8}$ in. under 21 in. But the Field Trial Springers are mostly much smaller than the show Springers, and very few of them will measure up to 20 in. Mr. Riddle records having measured F.T. Ch. "Staindrop Patricia ", who was exported to America, as measuring only $18\frac{3}{8}$ in.

CHAPTER V

BREEDING

ONE of the first things one is told when one talks of breeding is 'get the best bitch you can afford, as the bitch is the first essential foundation of a breeding kennel.' Who am I to dispute this? And yet I find that the longer I breed dogs the more I discover that there are no hard and fast rules to successful breeding. Any modest success I have had has not been the result of an exhaustive study of genetics, but has been composed of 50 per cent. commonsense and 50 per cent luck! So cheer up you beginners—you do not need untold wealth or a profound knowledge of genetics to breed that Champion!

Many beginners start the hard way by buying a well-bred bitch puppy of about eight weeks of age, then at her second or third heat they have her mated to one of the popular sires of the moment, and with bated breath they await the resulting litter hoping to be able to retain one or two winners; this is a long-term policy which may not work.

An easier way is to buy, or obtain on breeding terms, a proved brood bitch of really good pedigree. Study this pedigree carefully, and try to find a stud dog of the same strain, possibly with mutual grand parents, as this helps you to fix a type. If by any chance the bitch you buy has already been successfully mated previously and produced winners, you cannot do better

Plate VII

Six influential Springers in chronological order. (*top, left and right*) Ch. " Peter of Lorton Fell " and Int. Ch. " Advert of Solway " ; (*centre, left and right*) " St. Peter's Victoria " and " Peter's Benefactor " ; (*bottom, left and right*) Ch. " Bramhope Recorder " and Ch. " Duchess of Stubham ".

Plate VIII

Ch. " Stokeley Lucky ".

Photo by Mrs. M. Jones.

Ch. " Stokeley Bonn Boy ".

Int. Ch. " Frejax Royal Salute ".

Photo by May Studios.

than to repeat the previous mating, for it is more than likely that she will repeat her previous success.

To give you a classical example of this, I am sure Mrs. Kay Till will not mind my referring to her lovely bitch " Susan of Stubham ", her foundation bitch, who was mated at least six times to " Boxer " and in different litters produced Chs. " Alexander ", " Dinah ", " Duchess ", all ' of Stubham ', and other C.C. winners, including " Sheila " and " Amanda ". Sons and daughters of these dogs were then used to establish type and so a winning strain was evolved.

With this in mind I purchased " Clintonhouse Hazeltong Judith " from Mr. Davies, mated to his own dog " Colmaris Toreador ". (She had already bred Ch. " Colmaris Contessa ", to " Boxer ", Ch. " Clintonhouse George ".) Then she joined my kennels and I repeated the mating to " Boxer " and in one litter she produced Ch. " Bathsheba ", " Bowbell " (one C.C.) and " Bonavinto " all ' of Bramhope '.

If you cannot obtain a proved brood bitch, the next best thing is to put yourself in the hands of a reputable breeder who has a litter of puppies about seven or eight weeks old, and try to pick a sturdy, well grown, bold puppy. First watch them playing in the open, and when you have mutually decided on one you fancy, put it on a table and stand it up. At eight weeks old a Springer pup should be a replica of the finished product: head clean, not thick in skull, with reasonably dark eyes (most puppies eyes darken with age), short-coupled body, good bone, straight front legs with no looseness in the shoulder (put the finger between the shoulder blades, if set very wide apart this can mean loose shoulders), tail set low and not always carried high (many pups carry tails high when romping and playing with the rest of the litter, which may only be a sign of high spirits), nice flat coat of good texture, well-bent stifles, not too long from pastern to hock, and not turned inward (cow-hocked) or outward.

Ask the breeder's advice as to feeding and rearing your puppy. I believe in treating a young pup as one would a small child, giving regular meals, regular exercise, plenty of sleep and clean, airy surroundings. She should have been treated for worms before leaving the breeder, but if she appears pot-bellied after food, or has a ravenous unnatural appetite, a further worming at three months old is advisable. I use ' Ruby ' or Spratt's ' Red Mixture ' for this purpose, and have always had good results. I am a great believer in the daily garlic capsule too, to keep the bowels clean and prevent disease.

Plenty of raw meat every day with cod liver oil once or twice a week, raw eggs, shredded wheat, baked brown bread, tripe, sheep's paunches, green vegetables are all good feeding. My only ' don'ts ' are white bread and potatoes!

Most breeders have their puppies inoculated against the dreaded hard pad and distemper by a qualified veterinary surgeon, and although my own dogs are nature reared (that is daily garlic with raw foods, and so on) and build up their own immunity, I would not impose my views, and so always tell puppy buyers that if they are afraid of disease to have their pup inoculated as a precautionary measure.

MATING

An English Springer bitch can be safely bred from when she is about fifteen months old. Choose a good winning sire of similar blood lines, and preferably one

who has sired winning puppies already. Let the owner
of the sire know as soon as your bitch commences her
heat and make arrangements for your visit. If at all
possible your bitch will be happier if you are with her
for her 'marriage', but if the distance is too
great, do see that she has a comfortable box to travel
in, and never send her on a collar and chain only.
Immediately prior to the mating, see that both dog and
bitch have a run to empty themselves, and neither
should be fed for some hours previously. The stud fee
is payable at the time of service, and the usual agree-
ment in the case of a 'miss', is for a free service to
be given at the bitch's next heat.

Some bitches will stand naturally, turning the tail
and accepting the dog quietly, but many are snappy and
must be kept on a tight lead. Be guided by the owner
of the stud dog in this matter. I find that the eleventh or
twelfth day, counted from the first day the bitch has
shown signs of blood, are the most usual days for mating. No two bitches are alike in their behaviour at this
time, and stud dogs vary in their habits, so gentleness
and patience are always called for. Some stud dogs will
turn tail to tail as soon as they feel the tie complete,
others will wait for the assistance of their owner. Once
the tie is complete and the two dogs are tail to tail, the
owners should stand quietly holding them on the leads,
not fussing or petting them, but just making sure that
the bitch does not try to sit down or roll over, otherwise
the dog might be injured.

I usually have a bowl of cold water with a spot of
Dettol in it at the ready, and as soon as they break I
hold a pad of cotton wool soaked in the cold water to
the bitch's vulva, as I think this helps it to contract and
seal in the semen from the dog. I also sponge down the

dog's organs before putting him back in his kennel, and give him a bowl of raw egg and milk to eat. The bitch should then be put away in a quiet kennel for an hour and not allowed to romp about.

For the next five weeks normal good food and exercise is all that is needed for the bitch. Watch closely for any sign of worms, however, and if these are seen, dose for worms within the first fortnight of her pregnancy. The period of gestation is nine weeks from the date of mating, but where the litter is a large one the bitch may easily whelp three or four days early, or on the other hand if there should be only one or two pups she may go a couple of days or more over her time.

If she sleeps in a kennel with another dog she may be left as usual to within a fortnight of her whelping date, and then be placed in the kennel or place where you want her to whelp. A clean box, no less than 4 ft. by 3 ft., raised a couple of inches from the ground, with a loose rail all round the sides about 5 in. or 6 in. from the floor of the box to prevent her pressing up against the sides and maybe squashing a puppy, is the ideal box. When the pups are old enough (possibly at ten or eleven days) this rail can be removed.

I use an infra-red lamp (dull emitter, as a light disturbs the dam and prevents her sleeping) suspended on chains from the kennel roof. At first this can be placed about 3 ft. over the box and can gradually be raised as the pups develop and need less heat. The floor of the box may be lined with clean newspapers and a clean bed of wheat straw made ready for the whelping; then once the last pup has arrived, the bed can be cleaned out, wiped over with a weak solution of Dettol, and clean straw put down again.

WHELPING

Most bitches will let you know when they feel their babies are due, for they seem restless and often refuse their food. At this stage a brisk walk on a lead, not too far from home, is helpful. I have a cricket field next door to my kennels, and many are the miles I've walked round and round with my expectant mothers! While on this walk a sure sign that the time is near is a tendency for the bitch to pass water frequently; watch her closely for a gummy discharge from the vagina. Shortly after this discharge appears a small gelatinous water bag may protrude slightly, and now is the time to take her back to await events. (See Whelping Table on page 96.)

By this time she will be panting and uneasy. Some bitches like their owners to sit with them, others do better alone for a time. I usually leave my whelping bitch alone, then if she whines or barks, I take my stool, arm myself with clean newspapers, sterilized scissors, Dettol, and a bundle of cottonwool, and sit quietly with her. As the pains become fiercer she will pant more heavily, turning round and round and licking her vulva. As the pains increase in frequency she will commence to strain, and burst the water bag—the first puppy should be born within half an hour after this.

English Springer bitches are usually sensible whelpers and when the puppy appears in its little bag they will break this open with their teeth, sever the cord, and then proceed to lick the puppy vigorously to clean it up. Maiden bitches sometimes do not seem to know what has happened to them, and after ejecting the puppy take no further interest, it is then up to the owner to quickly remove the puppy from its bag, sever the cord about three inches from the body and pop the afterbirth into a newspaper, then rub the puppy dry with clean cotton wool, give it to the bitch and encourage her to clean and lick it. It is surprising how tough these babies are, and vigorous rubbing until the first little cry is heard can work wonders!

If the litter is a big one I usually offer the mother a warm drink of milk sweetened with glucose half way through her confinement. Often four or five puppies will be born at regular intervals, and then there may be a gap of an hour or more before she starts proceedings again—this seems to be Nature's way of giving the mother a rest.

Once you have seen all the puppies born and made sure they are suckling and are dry and warm, you can safely leave them all to have a good rest. Incidentally, you will feel like a good rest yourself as most pups seem to arrive during the night hours! If the litter is a big one I usually place a half-filled rubber hot water bottle, carefully wrapped in clean blanket under a corner of the straw, then while some of the pups are suckling the remainder can keep warm on this.

The following day the bitch will not require heavy meals. Milk and glucose or honey, milk puddings and so on are quite enough, as she will usually run a slight temperature. The next day milk foods and fish will be enough, and if all is well she can then go on to normal food. Raw meat is the best milk producer of all, while an egg broken on to it is a nourishing addition. After the first week she will be very hungry and should be fed more often than normally.

Should you find her neglecting her pups, being listless and not cleaning them up, it is advisable to send for the veterinary surgeon; he may give her an injection of penicillin into the vagina to kill any danger of septic infection.

I always keep a baby's feeding bottle handy and if there are any weakly or undersized pups I supplement their feeds with Ostermilk No. 2 with glucose added, and this is a help to the mother if her litter is a big one.

The mother will clean her babies thoroughly until they are about a fortnight old but after this they will need more of your attention. If the front of their box is hinged to form a ramp they will soon learn to stagger down and empty themselves on the clean sawdust of the kennel floor. For the first few days the dam will not want to leave her babies, but she must be taken out on a lead at regular intervals to relieve herself, after the first week she can be exercised as usual.

DOCKING AND DEW-CLAWS

At four days old the tails of the pups should be docked, and the dew-claws removed. Your veterinary surgeon will do this for you, but if you feel you would like to do this yourself, invest in some good docking scissors for the tail, sterilize the blades in boiling water before use, have a clean tin with some fine permanganate of potash crystals in it, quickly remove approximately one-third of the tail, keep hold of the cut end firmly between the fingers to stop any bleeding, and seal the cut by rubbing with the potash.

Use sharp sterilized nursing scissors for the dew-claws and make sure you cut out the root or they will grow again, rub a little potash into the cut and there will be no bleeding. I always go over the whole litter again afterwards and make quite sure there is no bleeding; if I see any blood I hold a wad of cotton wool dipped in the crystals over the wound until the bleeding stops.

CHAPTER VI

FEEDING

ADULT FEEDING

THE English Springer is not usually a fussy eater, and the adult dog does well on two meals per day. I find it most convenient to feed the main meal around mid-day, and this consists of from $1\frac{1}{2}$ lb. to 2 lb. of raw meat cut in pieces about two inches square. Once or twice a week a raw egg should be added to the meat feed, and during the cold weather a spoonful of 'Solvitax' cod liver oil should be added twice a week. The mid-day meal can be varied by feeding raw sheep's paunches, tripe, or raw herrings. I like to give this meal entirely raw, unadulterated by hound meal or any cereal food. Cereal food, hound meal, dried brown bread and so on can then be given for the evening meal.

A good pressure cooker is invaluable, and rough meat, sheep's heads, chicken giblets, rabbits and hares can be cooked until the bones are crumbly and the resulting mixture can be used to soak the meal or brown bread. This makes a grand feed for the evening meal. Of course it is up to the individual owner to plan his dog's meal times to suit his own convenience. Provided the dog is fed at regular times there is no harm done by reversing the feeding to raw meat in the evening and the cereal meal in the morning. Dogs love a regular schedule, and in fact soon let you know when it is feeding time!

Plate IX

Mr. I. Davies with Ch. "Clintonhouse George".

Ch. "Camdin Chief".

Sh. Ch. "Wallburn Wallflower".

Plate X

(left)

" Showman of Shotton ".

(below)

Am. Ch. " Melilotus Royal Oak ".

Photo by: Wm. Brown

Plate XI

(right)

"Northdown Donna".

(below)

"Boxer of Bramhope".

Photo by: Carlile Whitehead

Plate XII

Photo by]   [*Wm. Brown.*

Photo by]   [*Mornement*

Photo by]   [*Tauskey.*

Photo by]   [*Thurse*   Photo by]   [*A. G. Jones*

(*top left*) Am. Ch. " Kaintuck Beau Brummel " ; (*centre left*) Int. Ch. " Ascot's Ajax " ;
(*bottom left*) Sh. Ch. " Studley Brave Buccaneer " ; (*top right*) Sh. Ch. " Beauvallet of
Crosslane " ; (*bottom right*) Ch. " Stokeley Gay Boy ".

There are many good makes of biscuit meal on the market to-day, and these should be well soaked (but not sloppy) and allowed to cool before feeding. The addition of green vegetables may be beneficial too.

I save the outside leaves of cabbages, sprouts and so on, raw carrot and put them through the mincer once or twice a week and mix these in well with the biscuit meal. Onions make a tasty addition to the stew pot and act as a worm preventive. . . . they also act as a natural laxative, and should on this account only be used once or twice a week.

If a dog is fed on a good natural diet it should not need a lot of patent conditioners or medicines, but I would never be without ' Vetzyme ', a pure yeast product which all dogs seem to love, and in fact eat as a child eats sweets! They are a grand natural tonic for puppies and dogs of all ages.

Large bones given once or twice a week are good and help a dog's digestive organs, and act as a cleanser for the teeth, but small splintery bones such as chicken, rabbit or chop bones should never be given, as they may lodge in the throat, or in the intestines.

WEANING

I have already dealt with the feeding of the pregnant bitch in the chapter on breeding, so now I will go on to the all-important question of puppy feeding. The first six months of a puppy's life are the most important, and can make or mar your future show dog. For the first fortnight and up to three weeks the good dam should do all that is necessary for the feeding of her pups, and if the pups are quiet, eating and sleeping, then all is well. If however, they appear restless, and cry, it may be they need extra nourishment. If very young this means resorting to the feeding bottle and a good mixture of any of the baby foods sweetened with honey or glucose.

At about three weeks old the puppies can be taught to lap, at first once a day, and by the time they are four weeks old up to four times a day. At about four weeks they can be introduced to raw meat, a teaspoon at first increasing daily until at five weeks they can take a handful.

The meat should be scraped or minced very finely until they are about six weeks old, after that it should be chopped into small pieces.

At five weeks old they can also commence feeding on one of the puppy-grade biscuit meals, well soaked in good stock, and cod liver oil should be added to this. By the time they are six weeks old, weaning is nearly complete, and the bitch should be allowed to please herself as to whether she wants to feed them occasionally or not. From three weeks onwards she will want to be away from them more and more.

PUPPY FEEDING

At five or six weeks the mother may want to sleep alone, although she will possibly like to pay them a visit before bedtime, for a final lick round! Four feeds a day for the puppies are by no means too many at this stage and up to eight or nine weeks old, a normal schedule is as follows:

8.30 a.m.—Robinson's Barley Kernels, soaked in raw milk overnight and sweetened with honey, or shredded wheat and milk, or any of the children's cereals.

12 noon—raw meat. As I have already recommended, a raw egg can be occasionally broken on to the meat.

4 p.m.—milk pudding or cereal.

8 p.m.—puppy meal soaked in good stock and allowed to cool, with cod liver oil added.

Raw meal sweetened with honey is always a good drink at any time. Clean fresh drinking water should always be available for both dam and puppies, but see that the vessel is foolproof, as puppies are nosy little creatures and may fall in!

Don't be alarmed if you find that the dam is vomiting her meals for the puppies to eat, for many do this and it is only Nature's way of providing pre-digested food for the young. It can mean, however, that the dam herself may get insufficient nourishment, so if you see her making a regular habit of this, it is advisable to keep her away from her babies for several hours after her feed.

Puppies love large bones to gnaw, but watch carefully for any signs of fighting and never leave bones in the kennel overnight.

At three or four months old the meals can be cut down to three daily, and at six months to two daily, with the extra addition of a couple of hard brown rusks or good biscuits to chew in between.

A garlic tablet first thing every morning before food is the best internal disinfectant I know, and also helps to keep the puppies free from worms and skin troubles, in fact I always give a week's supply with any puppy I sell.

CHAPTER VII

GENERAL MANAGEMENT

THE English Springer Spaniel makes an ideal house dog, being faithful, kind in nature and loyal to his family. A good guard dog without being vicious, he is easily taught words of command, and will soon know his own resting place. A large dog basket away from draughts is ideal for him, or he may claim an old chair if you place his blanket on it. For the one dog owner there is no problem, but for the breeder with several dogs outside kennels are necessary.

KENNELLING

Good timber kennels are fairly expensive these days, and of course have a limited life of perhaps twenty or thirty years. Brick outbuildings or loose boxes make warm, draught-proof kennels. If these are used the dogs should have strong wooden sleeping boxes, raised three or four inches from the floor, open at the front, but with sides and tops to keep out the draughts. For bedding, clean wheat straw is good, although often difficult to obtain, oat straw is inclined to be dirty and to harbour insects. Fine wood wool is being used quite a lot these days, and is very good and clean for adult dogs, but I prefer wheat straw for puppy rearing, as the wood wool is inclined to be coarse and wind around the limbs of young puppies.

Stable-type doors are useful, as in warm weather the tops can be left open, bob-holes in the doors allow the dogs to go in and out at will, and save them wetting on the floors of the sleeping kennel. And access into covered or open runs enable the dogs to overcome boredom as they can always see what is going on in the outside world.

Concrete runs are easy to keep clean, and help to keep the tight cat-like feet which are so important in the breed, but if there is any danger of the dog sitting around, a strong wooden platform a few inches from the concrete should be placed in the run.

Fresh air and regular exercise are quite as important as good food. Besides, the English Springer is a hardy dog and rain and snow do not bother him, he can be exercised in all weathers and will thoroughly enjoy himself, as long as his bed is warm and dry he will come to no harm and does not need coddling. In addition to the individual runs, a large pen, either grass or concrete where, in fine weather, several dogs can be left to play together, is very useful, and saves the usually overworked owner a great deal of time and shoe leather! One must be sure that the dogs agree together, and it is never wise to leave keen stud dogs in the same run with their ' girl friends ', or a fight may ensue. Walks at regular times train the dogs to be clean in their habits, and also enables them to get used to the lead.

During wet weather plenty of clean dry sawdust on the floors of the kennels helps to dry the feet and keep the damp from soaking into the wooden floors. Every morning the old sawdust should be swept up, the floor cleaned down and the sawdust renewed. At one time wooden kennels were always treated with creosote inside and outside, but nowadays paints are manufactured suitable for kennels, and a light coloured paint helps to create a clean bright atmosphere, but of course needs going over every six months or so. Once a week the sleeping boxes can be brought out into the open and washed out with a detergent plus a little Jeyes or similar mild disinfectant, then dried out in the sun (if any!), clean bedding put in the box, the inside of the kennel wiped down—and back into it goes your Springer full of happiness at his nice clean bed. I love to see mine jump into the new straw, swirl it about and then flop down with a sigh of sheer contentment.

GROOMING

Grooming is another essential for good health. With only one dog this is easy and can be done daily. With a larger kennel it is quite a good plan to try to give one or two a good grooming every day in turn. A strong table of good size is necessary for this, of such a height that the owner need not bend the back—this is also a good way of getting a dog used to standing for exhibition.

You will need the following grooming tools:—

No. 6 Spratt's steel comb.

Pair of sharp scissors for trimming the feet.

Durham-Duplex stripper for stripping the loose hair on the inner and under side of the ears.

A pair of hairdresser's thinning scissors for thinning the thick hair under the jaw and sides of the neck.

Wire hound-glove with velvet back to remove the dead hair on the back and to give a nice polish to the coat—all available at your pet shop.

A good insect powder such as Pulvex should always be at hand, and a sharp watch kept for any sign of scratching. At certain times of the year the grasses and blackberry bushes harbour small parasites which cause intense irritation to a dog but regular dusting with a good insect powder will cure this in about three days. Young puppies seem particularly susceptible to lice and need to be carefully watched, as the puppy lice are one of the main sources of worms. If a dog is heavily infested a good bath in Kur-Mange, leaving the preparation in the coat without rinsing out is a good cure.

Always make sure the inside of your Springer's ears are clean and dry. Regular weekly attention to the ears, cleaning with cotton-wool soaked in a little witch hazel is a soothing cleanser, and will help to prevent canker of the ear as the dog gets older.

Noisy dogs are a nuisance to yourself and everyone else, and in built-up areas can lead to trouble with the neighbours. Early training is necessary and the youngsters must learn what the command 'No' means. Continual barking or whining *must* be stopped and I find a few sharp taps with a folded newspaper usually does the trick. I have never been able to discover why this is so, maybe the flapping noise of the paper is the reason, it certainly can't hurt the dog in any way.

Where several dogs are kennelled you will sometimes get what we call the 'Springer Chorus', this is when they all join in a peculiar howl, seemingly for no reason. I have even seen wee puppies in the nest put their heads back and join in; but usually a sharp word or a clap of the hands is enough for them to stop abruptly. I believe this is rather peculiar to our breed.

In case this happens during the night, my husband rigged up a 'Heath Robinson' device of wire attached to the bedroom window which trails over the garage roof to the roof of the kennels and is attached to two heavy wooden sticks—a pull on the wire rattles the sticks on the roof of the kennels, and silence prevails. . . . Necessity is indeed the mother of invention!

AILMENTS

Doggy ailments would need a whole chapter at least if not a whole book. Several good books are available on this subject, one of the best being *The Book of the Dog* published by Nicholson and Watson, and this has an excellent section on ' Accident and Disease: Nursing and Treatment ' by a veterinary surgeon.

If a dog or puppy is off his food, or has diarrhoea, the sensible thing to do is to take his temperature. For this you need a blunt headed half-minute thermometer. Stand the dog up and gently insert the blunt end into the rectum and hold it there while you count thirty slowly. A dog in normal health has a temperature of $101\frac{1}{2}°$ F.— if it should be more than a degree above normal it is a sure sign that something is wrong.

A dog with a temperature should be kept warm and quiet, food should be withheld and only clean water given to drink; the old adage of ' starve a fever ' is still a good one. If the fever still persists after twenty-four hours a veterinary surgeon should be sent for. If any sickness or vomiting appears a couple of tablets of milk of magnesia can do no harm, and if it is only a mild stomach upset, this may clear it up. A dog in his natural state would, if ill, find a dark quiet place, lie there quietly without eating and let Nature take its course. But of course we dog lovers fuss around, trying to tempt

Plate XIII

Sh. Ch. " Vanity
Fair of Stubham".

Sh. Ch. " Stokeley Sea
Sprite ".

Photo by Mrs. M. Jones.

Ch. " Mowgrain
Mr. Chips ".

Photo by Cooke.

Plate XIV

The Author with her Ch.
" Bathsheba of Bramhope ".

Photo by " Yorkshire Post ".

(left)
Miss Anne Beattie with Ch.
" Belarosa of Bramhope ".

(below)
Ch. " Bathsheba of
Bramhope ",
Mrs. Gwen Broadley (judge),
Mr. Reg Kelland
(President), and Ch.
" Inveresk Raider ".

Photo by Cooke.

our dog with all sorts of tasty morsels; and to please us he may try to eat the unwanted dainties and consesequently upset his tummy all the more.

Complete fasting is far more trying to the owner than to the dog himself who doesn't feel like food anyhow! How often one reads of dogs being trapped in pits and rocks and living without food for weeks, and emerging thin, but fit and healthy? Many breeders believe in one day's complete fasting per week for all their dogs, and say that this rests the stomach and keeps their dogs fit. I'm afraid I'm a bit too soft-hearted to do this every week, but I do do this every now and again.

With a long-eared breed like the Springer, it is essential to keep the inside of the ears very clean, and as I have already said, a regular once-a-week clean out with a swab of cotton-wool soaked in witch hazel should be enough to safeguard against canker of the ear; should canker develop your veterinary surgeon can supply a good cortisone ear lotion which is very effective.

Skin trouble is not prevalent in our breed, but eczema sometimes breaks out and it is difficult to clear. Overfeeding on starchy products is one of the usual causes of this complaint, and it is useless trying to cure it with various outside applications of ointments without first cleaning out the entire system. A couple of days without food, plenty of fresh water to drink with a dose of Epsom salts in water each night for three nights, followed with a raw meat diet should clear it out of his system. There are some lotions to apply to cool the affected parts, and again I believe that the newest one has a cortisone base. But a simple and harmless remedy is pure witch hazel, which is both cooling and has an astringent effect.

It is a good idea to keep a doggy medicine cupboard containing the following : —

Half-minute rectal thermometer.
Cheap quality cotton wool.
T.C.P. and Dettol disinfectants.
Castor oil.
Epsom salts.
Milk of magnesia (tablet or liquid).
Witch hazel.
Surgical spirit.
Nursing scissors.
Docking scissors.
Puppy worming oil.
Tapeworm capsules.
New-skin lotion for minor cuts.
Bandages and Sellotape for minor injuries.

CHAPTER VIII

Exhibiting

FIRST and foremost exhibiting should be fun! To enjoy it to the full a sense of humour is important; and the following little maxim is good to think of at all times: ' Teach me to win if I may—and if I may not win, then above all teach me to be a good loser '.

It is a good thing to join at least one of the breed clubs, and also a local canine society. These local clubs usually run monthly match meetings, which make a very good training ground for puppies and novice exhibitors. They are pleasant social affairs and one makes many friends at these informal gatherings.

Next in importance come the sanction shows and limited shows, confined to members of the various societies. No dog who has won the high honour of a Challenge Certificate is eligible to compete at these shows.

Then come the open shows, where, as the name reveals the competition is open to all, Champions and novices alike. During the summer months many are run in conjunction with the agricultural shows and given good weather can be most enjoyable affairs.

The championship shows are the top shows for competition, starting with the great Cruft's in February, and continuing all up and down the country until the end of November. The highest award is the Challenge Certificate, ' the big green card ' as we call it, which is given for the best dog and best bitch in each breed. These two winners then compete for Best of Breed, and all Best of Breed winners then parade for the final Best in Show of all breeds, the highest honour of all!

Before any dog can claim the title of Champion he must win at least three Challenge Certificates under three different judges, and in the case of an English Springer Spaniel, must also obtain a qualifying certificate at a recognized Field Trial. A recent Kennel Club rule now allows us to call a Springer a 'Show Champion' as soon as he has won his three Challenge Certificates, but for the full title and rank of Champion the qualifying certificate is still necessary. You should attend as many shows as you can. Both *Dog World* and *Our Dogs* advertise all the forthcoming shows, and these papers are invaluable for much interesting information pertaining to all doggy matters.

If a dog is trained from puppyhood to walk quietly on a lead, to heel, stand correctly, and allow strangers to touch him, he will soon take to the show ring. Practice standing him in an attractive pose for a few minutes whenever you groom him, and he will soon learn what is expected. Regular grooming gives a healthy shiny coat, and you should use the wire hound-glove with velvet backing for this purpose.

Springers are apt to grow very thick hair on the neck and this can spoil the appearance and give a short-necked effect; under the chin this can be removed with a good stripper, but on the top of the neck the thick hair must be carefully thinned out by finger and thumb, a slight dusting with powdered resin making the hair tacky and easier to pull.

All heavy hair on the inside and underside of the ears should be cleanly stripped out. Never use a knife or stripper on the body coat, as this will make the coat very rough and wavy in time. All loose hair between the toes should be removed to give the feet a clean cat-like appearance. It is a good plan to keep standing away from your dog as you groom him, and look carefully for tufts and hairs which spoil his clean outline and symmetrical appearance, plucking these out until you are satisfied that his outline pleases your eye.

Little and often is a good plan for grooming instead of a mad dash a couple of days before the show! But if the dog's coat is very dirty or dull, bath him the day before the show, using Silvikrin or Vaseline shampoo, while for dull coats a little Estolan tonic, well rinsed out imparts a nice bloom. If only the white parts need cleaning, a good chalk block is easier to handle than the various powders, and this should be well rubbed on the white fur and then thoroughly brushed out. Take this to the show with you for a last-minute clean up, but be careful not to scatter it around the hall or you will get black looks!

For the benched shows you will need a round leather collar and a benching chain to fasten your dog to the ring on the bench. Teach him to sit quietly on his bench, for a whining dog is a nuisance to you and to all around and you will not be popular with your neighbours. You will also need a good leather slip lead for taking him into the ring. Teach him to walk round the ring without pulling, and when you are called out for the judge to examine him, loosen this lead and let it lie loosely on the shoulders to give your dog a clean neck-line—a tight choked-up lead spoils the dog's head and expression and neck-line. A piece of biscuit, or liver, in your pocket as a bribe, helps to keep the dog's attention on his owner instead of on the other inmates of the ring!

It is a wise plan to keep one special bag for carrying your show requisites. These will probably be :

    comb
    hound-glove
    chalk
    dog blanket
    collar and chain
    drinking dish
    bottle of water or milk
    towel
    soap
    cotton wool
    bottle of diluted disinfectant

If the bag is large enough include a spare pair of comfortable shoes for yourself, as, believe me, a change of shoes can be heaven on a long day's dog showing!

Unless your dog is a very good traveller it is better not to feed before leaving home. An extra good feed the night before the show should keep him happy until he gets there, when you can always buy some dog biscuits or canned meat at the various stalls there. Try to give him every opportunity to empty himself before you go into the hall, and give him as many walks as possible during the day or he will feel uncomfortable and unhappy in the ring.

Give yourself plenty of time to get to the show, so that you are not dashing into the ring at the last minute —it's not fair either to the dog or yourself to be in a rush. Be ready at the side of the ring when your class is called in, when the ring steward will hand you your number, and you then stand your dog until the judge calls him out to examine him. Different judges have different methods, so just do what is asked of you and don't fuss your dog or he will sense your tension and will not do his best for you. If you are in more than one class, the ring steward will probably tell you where to stand in your next class.

If you are lucky enough to win a prize at your very first show, be happy, but don't imagine this win will always happen! No two judges think alike; you may meet different and better dogs; and again your dog may not always show as well; so learn to lose with a smile, and be assured that if your dog is good sooner or later it may be your turn to hold out your hand for the big green card!

Exhibitors on the whole are a grand bunch of folk, always ready to help a beginner and cheer him on when he does well. As in any walk of life you will always come up against the odd disgruntled exhibitor who whispers and sneers, but thank goodness, these are few and far between, and one soon learns to avoid them like the plague!

As soon as you leave the show, use your diluted disinfectant and sponge your dog's nose, mouth, and feet with this, to ward off any germs he may have gathered during the day, and wipe your own hands and shoes with disinfectant when you get home before going into your kennels to any young puppies or bitches with pups.

CHAPTER IX

TRAINING

MANY societies run obedience training classes. These are an excellent training ground, as obedience is so essential to Gundog training, and it is useless to gun-train until the dog is obedient to your commands. A dog who pulls and tugs on his lead is a nuisance, and an early lesson should be that of walking to heel on a lead. A slip lead is useful for this, and every time the dog pulls forward say 'Heel' sharply and tap his nose with a twig or folded newspaper until he realizes that he must not come forward. Again patience is needed, as I always find this one of the hardest lessons of all! Most pups object strongly to a lead at first, and it often helps to let them run about the yard for a short time every day with a cord around the neck to get used to the feel of it, before attempting the actual lead training.

I suppose it is a natural instinct for a Springer Spaniel to chase hens and livestock, but it is one which must be quelled at an early age. If he can be walked on his lead among poultry or sheep at an early age, and be taught 'No' every time he pulls forward or shows any interest, he will gradually get used to them, but never let him roam on his own without a lead or he will soon pick up bad habits and become a nuisance in the neighbourhood.

OBEDIENCE WORK

It is fairly easy to teach a puppy to sit: say the word 'Sit' and at the same time place your hand on his buttocks and press him down until he sits. When he has learnt that lesson try raising your hand at the same time as you give the command ' Sit ', and after a time he will learn to sit at the raised hand signal alone. This can be useful later on when he commences his training to the gun, and you wish him to sit without raising your voice.

Once he will sit to command you can try walking away from him. Of course he will immediately get up to follow you, but say ' No ', and take him back to where he was sitting, press him down and first say ' Sit ', and then ' Stay '. After time and patience he will learn to sit and stay when told, but this is a lesson which has to be repeated time and time again, each time taking him back to the original spot where you told him to sit.

All these lessons are reasonably easy to perform in a one-dog household, but in a breeding kennel with many young ones growing up all this individual attention is a very difficult matter. Little lessons have to be given while feeding and exercising, but the effort is well worth while.

It is well worth while making enquiries in your district to find out if there is a dog training society. In urban areas the police sometimes run police training schools for dogs. As well as being excellent training for the dogs, I believe the owners get a lot of fun out of it, and a lesson that can be boring when one is alone with one's dog, is great fun when competing with other people and other dogs. This contact with strange dogs is also good when contemplating a show career, as many puppies are overwhelmed with shyness at their first few shows— seeing so many strange folk and unusual dogs must be very bewildering to the puppy mind!

In spite of the new Kennel Club regulation whereby a Gundog can now receive the title of ' Show Champion ' as soon as he has won his three Challenge Certificates under three different judges, the elusive title of Champion can still only be obtained by winning a qualifying certificate at a recognized Field Trial in addition to the three green cards.

The English Springer Spaniel is a natural worker and exhibitors should not be deterred from making the attempt to achieve the title. Training begins at home, and can be done to start with in a room, so that even flat dwellers have no excuse!

Simple obedience can be commenced at three or four months, teaching the youngster to sit quietly by your chair. When he has learnt this have handy an old sock stuffed with cotton-wool and throw this to the far corner of the room and encourage the puppy to run and bring it to you. After he has done this a few times keep a firm hand on his neck when you throw it and say ' No ', keep him sitting quietly for a moment or so, then say ' Go fetch '. Reward him with a bit of biscuit and a pat when he has done this correctly a few times. If this is done for a few minutes every night in less than a week he should be looking forward to his game and be bringing the dummy tenderly to hand. When this lesson is learnt, you can hide the dummy behind the furniture and send him to find it—he will soon learn to use his nose and will enjoy the game of hide-and-seek.

Now is the time to commence a little training on his walks using exactly the same procedure as you did when indoors. If, in the excitement of the great outdoors, he runs away with the dummy and wants to play with it, do *not* make the mistake of running after him or he will think this is all part of the game, so call him to you and walk backwards away from him, when he will obey his natural instinct to come towards you with the dummy.

Once a lesson has been learnt, never keep on repeating it too often, or he will become bored with the whole procedure.

When all this has been learnt you can go a stage further, take somebody with you and get them to keep the puppy on a lead sitting quietly while you walk away trailing the dummy on a piece of cord. Go right out of the puppy's sight and trail the dummy behind a bush or in long grass, then walk back to him and say ' Hie lost ', at first he may run forward a few yards and then wait to see what you want of him, encourage him and go forward all the time saying ' Hie lost ', when eventually he should pick up the scent and start hunting. Encourage him with ' Good dog ', and ' Go fetch ', and as soon as he picks the dummy up, call him in to you, walking backwards again so that he brings it right up to your hand. Then encourage him to hunt in bushes and hedges, but try to keep him always within your control. Anybody with a reasonably intelligent puppy, provided they possess a certain amount of patience themselves, should soon have this simple training perfected.

FIELD WORK

If you possess a gun, a .410 or even an air gun, young puppies will get used to the sound of this around the place and will rarely be gun-shy. But never fire a gun at close range until you are quite sure that the youngster has no fear of the bang. Training pistols which fire blanks can be quite useful, but again should never be fired right over the dog's head; wait till the pup is way out hunting in front of you some distance and then fire. He will probably look up for a second and then go on hunting around. When you are quite sure he has no

fear of the bang, you can then go a stage further and
get a friend to fire the gun while you throw the dummy
and send the dog to retrieve it, always seeing that he
does not set off until you have given the command ' Hie
lost ' or ' Go fetch '.

Never lose your temper—patience and reward are all
that is needed. When he has got used to his first dummy,
you may be able to obtain a rabbit, skin it and hang the
skin in the sun to dry thoroughly, then stuff this and use
it instead of the old sock. Later you can try him on a
dead rabbit, then a pigeon, partridge or pheasant. If you
are lucky enough to be in a district where there is some
shooting, try to be around when this is going on to get
him used to the noise.

In order to teach him to hunt in the direction you
require try throwing the dummy to the left at the same
time motioning with your left arm in the direction you
have thrown the dummy (at the same time giving him
his usual ' Hie lost '), then to the right waving with the
right arm, and after a time he will learn to respond to
your arm signals moving to the left or right as required.
All this may sound fairly simple, but it is more difficult
than it sounds; it is your will against that of the dog's,
and believe me some dogs have mighty strong wills!

I hold a tremendous admiration for Mr. T. J. Greatorex of the ' O'Vara ' Field Trial Springers for his ease
of manner when handling his dogs at Field Trials. He
hardly raises his voice, uses very few hand signals or
whistles and yet his dogs respond as if by magic. It all
looks so simple and yet hours of patient training must go
into it all.

Field Trials are open to all as spectators, and I strongly
advise my show friends to spend a day at one or two

Trials to watch the work of the Field Trial dogs and their handlers. It really is most enjoyable and at the same time very instructive.

For show people who wish to run for a qualifying certificate for their Challenge Certificate winner the standard is not so high as for the Field Trial itself. The Qualifying Certificate reads as follows:

Qualifying Certificate

Kennel Club Field Trial Regulations require that all the Judges shall certify that any dog tested for a qualifying certificate fulfils the undernoted conditions, and we certify that the English Springer Spaniel ....
(name of dog) has fulfilled these requirements and is therefore granted a qualifying certificate.

Signed......(*name of judge*)

Signed......(*name of judge*)

Signed ...... (*name of secretary*)

Signed......(*name of secretary*)
     qualifying certificate.
(2) That the dog has been tested in the line.
(3) That the dog has shown that he is not gun-shy and was off the lead during gunfire.
(4) For a Spaniel, that he hunts, faces covert and retrieves tenderly.

Serious gun training should begin at about eight months old, when, if the obedience and simple retrieving practices have been really well carried out on the youngster, the real thing should not prove too difficult.

CHAPTER X

GLOSSARY OF TERMS

Affix   That which is attached to a dog's registered name in order to identify him with a particular kennel. It may consist of words added before or after the dog's name, and may be a prefix or a suffix, that is, for example, " Bingoland Buster " or " Buster of Bingoland ". For the sole right to use a certain affix, application has to be made to the Kennel Club, and a fee of one guinea per year made for the sole right to use this affix in Great Britain.

A.V. Stands for ' Any Variety ', a definition for classes at shows or stakes at Field Trials, showing that different varieties of dogs may compete.

B. of B. Best of Breed. A dog or bitch who has beaten all others of his breed.

Blaze. The white marking, usually running from nose to forehead—a nice straight blaze enhances the appearance of the head.

Bloom. Glossiness, an indication of a healthy coat with a good sheen.

Bone. Good bone in an English Springer's limbs is essential for show and work, gives an appearance of straight limbs and strength, but should never be coarse.

Breeder. The owner of the dam at the time of whelping.

Brace. Two dogs exhibited together.

Brisket. The chest, particularly that part between the forelegs and immediately behind them; good depth of brisket gives the heart and lung room so essential in a working dog.

B.I.S. Best in Show. A dog who has beaten all others.

B.O.S. Best of Sex. A dog who has beaten all others of his sex.

Butterfly Nose. Parti-coloured nostrils or flesh-coloured markings on the nose. This deters from the appearance of the head and is considered a serious show fault in some countries. Usually due to an iron deficiency in the blood. A course of Parrishes food or seaweed powder often has good results.

Cat-feet. Round, firm cat-like feet with tight toes, not open or splayed.

C.C. Challenge certificate. Large green-and white prize card awarded by the Kennel Club at championship shows for the best dog and best bitch in the breed.

Ch. Champion. The title awarded to a dog holding three Challenge Certificates awarded and signed by three different judges at championship shows, and a qualifying certificate awarded at a recognized Field Trial

Character. Showing brains, intelligence and the sweet disposition necessary to the Springer Spaniel.

Cloddy. Low and thick-set, having a clumsy appearance.

Cobby. Compact and short coupled—a cobby Springer might lack elegance.

Couplings. That part of the body between the shoulders and hips.

Cow-hocked. When the hocks turn inwards towards each other. A bad fault.

Dam. The mother of puppies.

Dew-claws. The claw of the fifth digit on the inside of the legs above the foot. This should be removed on the fourth day after birth.

Dewlap. The loose skin under the throat which if heavy and pendulous gives a nasty appearance and a throaty look.

Down in Pastern. A weakness in the foot giving a flat-footed appearance.

Dual Ch. Dual Champion. A dog who has won both the title of Champion on the bench and Champion at Field Trials.

Dudley Nose. Wholly flesh-coloured nostrils.

Feather. The long hair on the back of the legs and under the body. Good feathering adds greatly to the beauty of the Springer.

Flat-sided. Sometimes called slab-sided. Where the ribs are flat instead of well rounded with plenty of heart room. A bad fault in a Springer.

Flews. The pendulous lips. A nice depth of flew is desired but too heavy flews give a Bloodhound appearance to the head.

Front. As it implies the front of the Springer below his head, featuring his depth of brisket and straight legs.

F.T.Ch. Field Trial Champion.

Gay Tail. A tail carried high in a Terrier-like manner. A bad fault if habitually held in this manner, particularly in a bitch; a keen stud dog is sometimes

Plate XV

Sh. Ch.
" Hazel of Stubham ".

Photo by Fall.

m. Ch. " Melilotus
Shooting Star ".

Photo by Fall.

Ch. " Alexander
of Stubham ".

Photo by Anning.

Plate XVI

Scarborough Newspapers.

Sh. Ch. " Grand Lodge " (*above left*) and Mrs. Fradkish with
Ch. " Colmaris Chancellor ".

Sport and General.

Mrs. E. Beale and a litter by her " Racedale Rover ".

inclined to carry his tail gaily when in the company of other dogs, but if the tail is high set this is a fault.

Good Doer.   A dog with a good appetite who thrives well.

Hare-foot.   A long narrow foot with the toes well separated like those of a hare, and objectionable in a Springer.

Haw.   The red inner part of the lower eyelid. When a Springer's lower eyelids droop he shows this inner lining which spoils the expression.

Heat.   The term used to denote the six-monthly season of a bitch.

Height.   Usually the measurement from the ground to the top of the shoulder.

Hock.   The joint on the hind limb below the stifle.

Inbreeding.   The mating of very closely related dogs, such as mother and son, father and daughter, or brother and sister.   This can be a dangerous practice if any dominant faults are in the strain; although many experienced breeders have bred good ones this way it is not advised for novice breeders.

Int. Ch. International Champion.   A dog who has gained the title of Champion in more than one country.

Junior Warrant.   Owners of dogs who win twenty-five or more points in first prizes in classes for the breed at championship or open shows before they are eighteen months old, can apply to the Kennel Club for a junior warrant. A first prize at a championship show in the breed counts three points and a first prize at an open show in the breed class counts one point.

K.C.S.B. *Kennel Club Stud Book.* If a dog or bitch wins first, second or third in a limit or open class at a championship show, or a prize or award at a Field Trial, he qualifies for entry in this Stud Book, and thereafter the number in the Stud Book precedes his K.C. registration number on all pedigrees and documents. It is also possible under certain conditions to obtain entry by payment of a fee to the Kennel Club.

Leather. The skin of the ear flap, which in an English Springer often can be measured to the tip of the nose. If too short it gives the appearance of a Welsh Springer, while if too long gives a Cocker look to the head.

Leggy. Too high on the leg.

Level Jaws. When the teeth meet evenly, neither undershot nor overshot.

Loaded in Shoulder. When too much flesh is carried on the shoulders, giving a heavy appearance.

Litter. A family of puppies.

Long Cast. Too long in couplings. In an English Springer Spaniel the length from set-on of shoulders to the set-on of the tail should not be greater than the height from the ground to the set-on of the shoulder.

Maiden. The name given to a bitch who has never been mated. In show definitions it is given to a dog or bitch who has never won a first prize.

Match. Meetings held by canine societies at which dogs of different breeds are matched in competition against each other.

Muzzle.   The part of the head consisting of the mouth and nose.

N.A.F.   Name applied for.   This has to be inserted on entry forms when the dog is entered before the official registration has come through from the Kennel Club.

N.F.C.   Not for Competition. Inserted on entry forms when a dog is entered for a show, but is not competing for prizes.

Occiput.   The peak of the skull, which should not be pronounced in the Springer.

Oestrum.   The period of season or heat in a bitch.

Out at Elbows.   When the elbows are carried away from the chest wall and point outwards—a fault in the breed.

Out at Shoulders.   When the shoulders appear loose, and the front has a Bulldog effect.

Overshot.   When the upper jaw projects over and beyond the lower, sometimes called pig-jaw.

Pad.   The under portion of the foot which forms a cushion.

Pastern.   The lower part of the leg.

Quality.   A term meaning having a well-bred appearance.

Racy.   Usually used to denote a lean, rather leggy dog.

Roach Back.   An arched back, and a fault in the Springer.

Second Thigh.   The muscles immediately below the stifle, tapering toward the hock.

Service.   A mating between dog and bitch.

Shelly.   A thin, narrow, poorly-developed body.

Short Coupled.   Short in back and loins.

Sire.   A male parent.

Stern.   The tail.

Stifle.   The joint of the hind leg corresponding to the human knee.

Stop.   The indentation between and in front of the eyes, which should be pronounced in a Springer. When the stop is absent it gives a plain appearance to the head similar to that of the Bull Terrier.

Throatiness.   Too much dewlap or loose skin under the throat.

Tricolour.   Three colours in a Springer can be black white-and-tan, or liver white-and-tan.

Type.   That quality in a Springer which indicates that he is near to the standard laid down for the breed, in other words typical of the breed.

Undershot.   When the front of the lower jaw protrudes beyond the upper jaw, and a bad fault in the breed.

Upright in Shoulder.   Straight in shoulder, not sloping back enough.

Unsound.   Describes a dog with structural defects, or one who is lame or moves incorrectly through faulty bone structure.

Weedy.   A thin, scraggy, undernourished dog.

Whelping.   Another name for parturition, or giving birth to puppies.

Whelps.   An old fashioned name for puppies in the nest.

Withers.   The top of the shoulder where a dog is measured for height.

CHAPTER XI

ANTRIM AND DOWN ENGLISH SPRINGER
SPANIEL CLUB: Secretary, Mrs. McGladery, 2
Waterloo Park, Belfast, Ireland.

ENGLISH SPRINGER SPANIEL CLUB: Secretary,
Mrs. I. B. Hampton, Ebrington Hill, Chipping
Camden, Glos. This is the parent club of the breed.

ENGLISH SPRINGER SPANIEL CLUB OF
NORTHERN IRELAND: Secretary, H. A. Wilson,
Esq., The Hill, Cross Road, Lambeg, Co. Antrim,
Ireland.

ENGLISH SPRINGER SPANIEL CLUB OF SCOT-
LAND: Secretary, Mrs. C. Thompson, Over
Linkins, Castle Douglas, Scotland.

LONDON AND HOME COUNTIES ENGLISH
SPRINGER SPANIEL SOCIETY: Secretaries,
Mr. and Mrs. H. Kilby, 24 Blundell Road, Luton,
Beds.

MIDLAND ENGLISH SPRINGER SPANIEL
SOCIETY: Secretary, Mrs. M. Smithson, 'Studley', Royd Moor Lane, Hemsworth, Pontefract.

*In addition to the above specific breed
clubs there are a number of societies
which cater for Spaniels generally, and
these have always been very helpful to
the novice who is far away from the district assisted by a specialist club.*

EASTERN COUNTIES SPANIEL CLUB: Secretary, Miss D. Morland Hooper, 3 Eastfield Road, Royston, Herts.

NORTHERN AND MIDLANDS SPANIEL CLUB: Secretary, J. Owen, Esq., 303 East Lancs Road, Swinton, Lancs.

NORTH OF ENGLAND SPANIEL CLUB: Secretary, Mrs. O. McKeown, 46 Elsdon Street, Sunderland, Co. Durham.

SCOTTISH SPANIEL CLUB: Secretary, A. R. Anderson, Esq., 25 Lewis Street, Stranraer, Scotland.

SPANIEL CLUB: Secretary, T. J. Greatorex, Esq., Corndean, Hodnet, Shropshire.

WESTERN COUNTIES AND SOUTH WALES SPANIEL CLUB: Secretary, H. T. Davis, Esq., The Cottage, 69 Durleigh Road, Bridgwater, Somerset.

CHAPTER XII

TABLE OF REGISTRATIONS FROM 1919-1958

1919	...	29	1939	...	608
1920	...	156	1940	...	207
1921	...	394	1941	...	182
1922	...	690	1942	...	386
1923	...	1,122	1943	...	779
1924	...	1,208	1944	...	1,326
1925	...	1,432	1945	...	2,035
1926	...	1,256	1946	...	3,250
1927	...	1,328	1947	...	3,172
1928	...	1,271	1948	...	2,740
1929	...	1,229	1949	...	2,327
1930	...	1,104	1950	...	2,316
1931	...	1,017	1951	...	1,669
1932	...	942	1952	...	1,458
1933	...	927	1953	...	1,398
1934	...	996	1954	...	1,376
1935	...	1,075	1955	...	1,341
1936	...	1,085	1956	...	1,328
1937	...	1,066	1957	...	1,305
1938	...	1,149	1958	...	1,477

There we have forty years of English Springer Spaniel registrations with the Kennel Club, from the end of the First World War up to 1958. The figures speak for themselves, and particularly refreshing is it to see that the decline of the past decade has been arrested.

May this belated revival of interest in the breed be stimulated . . . and we are happy to be producing this the first book on the breed in Britain by a known authority in the very year following the turn of the tide.—*Editor*.

TABLE SHOWING WHEN A BITCH IS DUE TO WHELP

Served Jan.	Whelps March	Served Feb.	Whelps April	Served March	Whelps May	Served April	Whelps June	Served May	Whelps July	Served June	Whelps Aug	Served July	Whelps Sept.	Served Aug	Whelps Oct.	Served Sept.	Whelps Nov.	Served Oct.	Whelps Dec.	Served Nov.	Whelps Jan.	Served Dec.	Whelps Feb.
1	5	1	5	1	3	1	3	1	3	1	3	1	2	1	3	1	3	1	3	1	3	1	2
2	6	2	6	2	4	2	4	2	4	2	4	2	3	2	4	2	4	2	4	2	4	2	3
3	7	3	7	3	5	3	5	3	5	3	5	3	4	3	5	3	5	3	5	3	5	3	4
4	8	4	8	4	6	4	6	4	6	4	6	4	5	4	6	4	6	4	6	4	6	4	5
5	9	5	9	5	7	5	7	5	7	5	7	5	6	5	7	5	7	5	7	5	7	5	6
6	10	6	10	6	8	6	8	6	8	6	8	6	7	6	8	6	8	6	8	6	8	6	7
7	11	7	11	7	9	7	9	7	9	7	9	7	8	7	9	7	9	7	9	7	9	7	8
8	12	8	12	8	10	8	10	8	10	8	10	8	9	8	10	8	10	8	10	8	10	8	9
9	13	9	13	9	11	9	11	9	11	9	11	9	10	9	11	9	11	9	11	9	11	9	10
10	14	10	14	10	12	10	12	10	12	10	12	10	11	10	12	10	12	10	12	10	12	10	11
11	15	11	15	11	13	11	13	11	13	11	13	11	12	11	13	11	13	11	13	11	13	11	12
12	16	12	16	12	14	12	14	12	14	12	14	12	13	12	14	12	14	12	14	12	14	12	13
13	17	13	17	13	15	13	15	13	15	13	15	13	14	13	15	13	15	13	15	13	15	13	14
14	18	14	18	14	16	14	16	14	16	14	16	14	15	14	16	14	16	14	16	14	16	14	15
15	19	15	19	15	17	15	17	15	17	15	17	15	16	15	17	15	17	15	17	15	17	15	16
16	20	16	20	16	18	16	18	16	18	16	18	16	17	16	18	16	18	16	18	16	18	16	17
17	21	17	21	17	19	17	19	17	19	17	19	17	18	17	19	17	19	17	19	17	19	17	18
18	22	18	22	18	20	18	20	18	20	18	20	18	19	18	20	18	20	18	20	18	20	18	19
19	23	19	23	19	21	19	21	19	21	19	21	19	20	19	21	19	21	19	21	19	21	19	20
20	24	20	24	20	22	20	22	20	22	20	22	20	21	20	22	20	22	20	22	20	22	20	21
21	25	21	25	21	23	21	23	21	23	21	23	21	22	21	23	21	23	21	23	21	23	21	22
22	26	22	26	22	24	22	24	22	24	22	24	22	23	22	24	22	24	22	24	22	24	22	23
23	27	23	27	23	25	23	25	23	25	23	25	23	24	23	25	23	25	23	25	23	25	23	24
24	28	24	28	24	26	24	26	24	26	24	26	24	25	24	26	24	26	24	26	24	26	24	25
25	29	25	29	25	27	25	27	25	27	25	27	25	26	25	27	25	27	25	27	25	27	25	26
26	30	26	30	26	28	26	28	26	28	26	28	26	27	26	28	26	28	26	28	26	28	26	27
27	31	27	1	27	29	27	29	27	29	27	29	27	28	27	29	27	29	27	29	27	29	27	28
28	1	28	2	28	30	28	30	28	30	28	30	28	29	28	30	28	30	28	30	28	30	28	1
29	2	29	3	29	31	29	1	29	31	29	31	29	30	29	31	29	1	29	31	29	31	29	2
30	3			30	1	30	2	30	1	30	1	30	1	30	1	30	2	30	1	30	1	30	3
31	4			31	2			31	2			31	2	31	2			31	2			31	4

INDEX

" Admiration of Solway ", Ch., 25

" Advert of Solway ", Int. Ch., 25, Pl. vii

Ailments, 70-72

Aldridges, 11

Aldrovandus, Ulysses, 2

" Alexander of Stubham ", Ch., 38, 39, 40, 41, 42, 55, Pl. xv

" Alwinton Faithful Maid ", 36

" Amanda of Stubham ", 39, 55

" Ambergris Alert ", 31, 36

" —— Harvester ", 32

American Kennel Club, 51

Anderson, E. A., 38, 40, 43

Arkwright, William, 6, 7, 9

" Artist's Model ", 28

" Artistry Raffles ", 41

" Ascot's Ajax ", Int. Ch., Pl. xii

Ashton, Ellis, 15

Audemer, Pl. iv

Austin, Miss Prudence, 38

" Bambino of Bramhope ", 42

" Banchory Bright ", F.T. Ch., 14

" —— Flame ", F.T. Ch., 14

" —— Gloss ", 14

" Banker of Bramhope ", 42

" Banner of Beechfield ", 37

" Barnadine of Bramhope ", 46

" Bathsheba of Bramhope ", Ch. 41, 43, 46, 55, Pl. xiv

Beagle, 8

" —— of Bramhope ", 41, 42

Beal, Mrs. D., 39

Beale, Mrs. E., Pl. xvi

" Beanmore Camdin Greta ", Ch. 40

Beattie, Miss Anne, Pl. xiv

" Beauchief Barham ", Ch., 28

" —— Benefactor ", Ch., 15, 16, 19, 24

" Beauchief Bonnetta ", Ch., 15

" —— Buchanan ", Ch., 15

" —— Lady Barbara ", 15

" —— Major ", 15, 16

" —— Nicholas ", 15, 16

" —— Outcross ", Ch., 28

" Beautility Brocade ", 34

" Beauvallet of Crosslane ", Sh. Ch., 43, 44, Pl. xii

" Beechgrove Donaldson ", Ch., Pl. vi

" —— Will ", Ch., 7

" Belarosa of Bramhope ", 24, 40, 41, 43, 46, Pl. xiv

Bell, Mrs. H. M. S., 39, 46

" Bell ", 24

" Betty of Highedge ", 19, 28

" Birkdale Beggarmaid ", 37

Black, W., 40

Blake, Victor, 16

Blakey, Pl. iii

Blome, Richard, *Frontispiece*

" Boghurst Berry ", 16

" —— Bristle ", Ch., 16

" —— Carlo ", 16

" —— Rover ", 16

Bolton, J., 37, 38

" Bonaventure of Bramhope ", 42, 44, 45

" Bonavinto of Bramhope ", 55

" Bonnie Wee Teal ", 43, 44

Book of the Dog, The, 70

Boughey family, 3

Boughton, Sir W. Rouse, 17

" Bountiful of Beechfield ", 37, 40

Bowers, T. B., 6

" Bowbell of Bramhope ", 43, 45

" Boxer of Bramhope ", 14, 2 32, 34, 37, 39, 42, 43, 53, 55, Pl. xi

" Bracken of Crosslane ", 38

Braddon, Joe, 31, 32, 33, 34,

" Bramble Amber ", 40

" Bramhope Recorder ", Ch., 37, 39, Pl. vii

" Bramhope Suzette ", 25
" Brandyhole Bellflower ", 41
" —— Berry Brown ", 44, 46
Breeding, 54-61
Broadley, Mrs. Gwen, 28, 32, 33, 34, 35, 36, 37, Pl. xiv
Broughall, Mrs. Basnett, 11
" Brown Bess of Bramhope ", 44, 46
" Brownie ", 9
" Bryngarw Coloraine ", F.T. Ch., 16
" —— Firearm ", F.T. Ch., 16
" —— Firefly ", F.T. Ch., 16
" —— Firelight ", F.T. Ch., 16
" —— Jock ", F.T. Ch., 16
" Burleeds Brigadier of Bramhope ", 38, 42
Burns, Robert, 20
Burton, F. J., 6, 35, 41, 43
Byrne, A., 26

Caius, John, 1, 2, Pl. i
" Caliph of Malwa ", Int. Ch., 16
" Camdin Chief ", Ch., 39, 41, Pl. ix
" —— Mistress Lucy ", 39
Campbell, D., 40
Campion, Mrs. R., 46
" Candida of Crosslane ", 40
Cane, R. Claude, 7
" Canfordborne Dream Girl ", 28
" —— Mediant ", Ch., 28
" —— Vivace ", 28
" Canonite Powder ", 9
" Carnfield Albvic Legioner ", 34
" —— Cadet ", 17
" —— Christabelle ", Ch., 32, 39
" —— Chick ", Ch., 34, 39
" —— Field Marshall ", 30, 34
" —— Florrie ", 35
" —— King ", 17
" —— Lily ", 17
Carrell, Lt-Col. F. B. H., 18, 31
Carter, A. W., 18
" Castlecary Cameronian ", Ch., 36

" Castlelea Squadronaire ", 44
" Cavehill Maid ", 35
Charlesworth, Mrs. W. M., 23
" Charming of Chastleton ", 30
Chassels, A. McNab, 15, 16, 20, 21, 31
" Chastleton Lucky Lady ", 39
" —— Waxwing ", 35
Chevrier, 27
Chronicles, Froissart's 1
Church, W., 16
Cinema, Peaceful night in a, 23
Clark, Mrs. R., 44
" Claxton Outspan ", 34
Cleland, Bob, 32, 34
" Clintonhouse Elizabeth ", 34
" —— George ", Ch., 28, 38, 39, 40, 41, 43, Pl. ix
" —— Hazeltong Judith ", 28, 39, 55
Clubs, 92-93
Cock-Spaniel, 5
Cocker Spaniel Handbook, The, 11
" Colmaris Chancellor ", 44, 45, Pl. xvi
" —— Contessa ", 39, 40, 41, 44, 55
" —— Nice Fella ", 45
" —— Tawny Jewel ", 43
" —— Toreador ", 35, 39, 55
" Come Back ", 32
Complete Farrier, The, 5
" Conquest of Clyne ", 42
Cooper, Miss Helen, 46
Cornthwaite, R., 25
" Corrin of Gerwin ", 7
" —— —— Gerwn ", 7
Crawford, G. G., 36, 46
Cripps, Miss Betty, 37
Cudworth, T., 43
Cupit, Miss Dorothy, 31, 32, 36
Cynographia Britannica, Pl. iii

Dachshund, 8
" Dalshangan Dandy Boy ", F.T. Ch., 17
Daniel, 8
" Dash ", 24
" —— II ", 7

Davies, I., 35, 38, 39, 40, 44, 45, 55, Pl. ix
Davy, F. L., 36
Dawson, F., 46
——, Mrs. R., 39
De Canibus Britannicis, 1, Pl. i
de Foix, 1
" Deana of Glenbervie ", 38
" Denne Duke ", Ch., 11
Derbyshire Sheepdogs , 15
Devonshire, Duke of, 15
Dew-claws, 61
Dewhirst, Miss Gillian, 46
Diamond, Mrs. M. L., 45
"Diamond Powder ", 9
Dick, Hon. Mrs. Quintin, 18
" Dilkusha Punch ", 21
" Dinah of Stubham ", Ch., 39, 55
" Dinsdale Dame ", 37
" —— Donna ", 39
Dinwoodie, Mrs. Tom, 37
Dobson, Mrs. G., 46
Docking, 61
Dog Book, The, 4
—— *World,* 74
Dooley, S., 43
" Dovehouse Wonder Boy ", 45
" Downton Darkie ", 17
" —— Duchess ", 17
" —— Flash ", 17
" —— Tinker ", 17
Doyne- Ditmas, Maj. H. E. C., 16
Drentsche Patrijshond, Pl. iv
" Drumcree Joan ", 34
" Dry Toast ", Ch., 30
" Dryburgh Thistle ", 44
" Duchess of Stubham ", Ch., 43, 44, 55 , Pl. vii
Dudgon, E. W., 35
Dumont, Robert, 12
Durie, Mrs. Campbell, 45
" Duskie Princess ", 45, 46

Eagle on the shoulder , 19
Earl, Maud, Pl. v
East William, 9, 31
——, (His poem ' To

Tetton '), 10
Eczema, 71
Edward VI, 1, 2
Edwards, Mrs. Mollie, 47
——, Sydenham, Pl. iii
——, W. D., 23, 24
Elizabeth I, 2
English Setter Handbook, The, 19
" Eriska of Kilduskland ", 46
E.S.S.C., 16, 19, 22, 27, 28, 31, 32, 36, 51
E.S.S.C.N.I., 32
E.S.S.C.S., 51
E.S.S.F.T.A., 12
Evans, 40
——, J., 43
Eversfield, C. C., 9, 11
Exercise, 67
Exhibiting, 73-77

Falconry, 19
Falcons, 19
" Fansome ", 7
Farrow, James, 4
Faults, 51, 52
Feeding, Adult, 62-63
——, Pregnant bitch, 60, 61
——, Puppy, 64-65
Field Trials, 6, 19, 80, 82, 83
—— work, 81-84
Findley, W., 46
" Fireflash ", 14
First-aid kit, 72
Fitz-Herbert, Sir Hugo, 3, 9
Flat-coated Retriever, 15
Fleming, Abraham, 2
" Flint of Avendale ", Dual Ch., 14, 27
" Follow Through of Solway ", Ch., 25
" Foxglove of Stubham ", 41
Francis, Miss C. M., 18, 19, 35, 41, 42
Frankish, Mr. and Mrs. H., 40, 44, 45, Pl. xvi
" Frejax Royal Salute ", Int. Ch., 33, 53, Pl. viii
Froggatt, Arthur, 47
——, Ernest, 37, 39, 47
Froissart, 1
Fussey, Mrs. A., 47

Gardiner, W. R., 35
Gardner, J. P., 11
Garlic, Value of, 65
Gaunt, Tom, 14
*Gentleman's Recreation, Front-
tispiece*
George, Mrs. D. L., 46
" Georgina of Harting ", 18
Gibson, J., 31
Glossary of Terms, 85-91
*Golden Retriever Handbook,
The,* 23
Goodger, Mrs. W Swainston,
14
" Grand Lodge ", Sh. Ch., 34,
35, 37, Pl. xvi
Grant, Rod, 39
Greatorex, T. J., 26, 82
Grierson, R., 25
Grooming, 68-69
" Groompy of Harting ", 18
" Guy of Gerwyn ", 7

Hamilton and Brandon, Duke
of, 11, 13, 14
Hampton, Ian, 31
——, Mrs. O. M. C., 31, 38, 43
Hannah, D. C., 34, 38, 44
Hanning, Miss Hilary, 36
——, Jimmy, 36, 41
Hare-Dinsley, Mrs. G. B., 47
Hartley, Mrs. G. B., 47
Harwell, George, 30, 31, 34
" Hazel of Stubham ", Sh. Ch.,
40, 41, Pl. xv
Hearnshaw, 6
" Hemlington Kalgar ", 18, 25
Hepplewhite, W. Rankin, 32,
33, 37
" Higham Barney Blazer ", 42
" —— Teal ", Ch., 18, 19
" —— Thyme ", 19
" —— Ticket ", 19
" —— Tom Tit ", Ch., 18
" —— Topsy ", 35, 41
" —— Tristram ", 33
" Highedge Keeper ", 19
" —— Minnie ", 19
Hill, Frank Warner, v, 14, 15,
16, 31
Hodgkin, A. C., 47
Honey, Value of, 60, 64, 65

" Honour of Harting ", 18
Hooper, Miss Morland, 24, 31
" Hopeful Judy ", 28
Horsbrugh, Major A. M., 35
" Horsford Hetman ", Dual Ch.,
20
" —— Honeybell ", 13
Howard, Mrs. H., 21, 30, 37, 39
Howe, Rt. Hon. Lorna Coun-
tess, 14, 18
Hubbard, Clifford, v, 19
Humphrey, William, 19, 32
Hungers Prevention, 2, 3
Hunt, H., 37

" Ideal Stamp ", 37
Illustrated Book of the Dog,
Pl. v
Infra-red lamp, 58
" Invader of Ide ", Ch., 32, 33,
34, 35, 39
" —— —— Ware ", 38, 39
"Inveresk Chancellor", Int. Ch.,
20
" —— Coronation ", Ch., 15,
Pl. vi
" —— Raider ", Ch., Pl. xiv
"Inverruel Raider", Ch., 40, 42,
44
" Invincible George ", 28
Ireland, Dr. Aubrey, 37

Jackson, Fred, 33
" Jambok of Ware ", Int. Ch.,
15, 27
" Jamson of Ware ", 21, 27
" Jess of Moncrief ", Ch., 35
" —— —— Shelcot ", Ch., 28,
32
" Jessica of Stubham ", 41, 43
" Jet of Chastleton ", 37
Johnson, G. A., 46
——, Mrs. M. M., 46
Johnston, W. R., 34, 44
Jones, G., 47
——, Harry, 7, 9
——, K., 47
——, Selwyn C., 26
" Julia of Hatherley ", 45

" Kaintuck Beau Brummel ",
Am. Ch., Pl. xii

Kelland, R. R., 22, Pl. xiv
Kennel Club, 7, 13, 17, 74, 80, 83
Kennel Club Stud Book, 7, 18
—— *Gazette*, 4
Kennelling, 66-68

Labrador Retriever, 14
Labrador Retriever Handbook, The, 42
Lambe, Lady Angela, 19, 31, 33, 34, 35, 36, 37, 38, 39, 43, 44
Lancashire, Mrs. B., 45
" Larkstoke Skylark ", 38
" —— Sugarcandy ", 43
Latham, J. Roster, 28
" Laverstoke Pancake ", 21
" —— Pattern ", Ch., 21
" —— Pedro ", 21
" —— Pepper ", Ch., 21
" — —Pilate ", 21
" —— Sapphire ", 21
Lawrence, Richard, 5
Lewis, J. Glyn, 41, 43
" Leymor Binx Bin ", 31,33
" —— Recorder ", 36
" Light of Ashleigh ", Ch., 36, 38
" L'ile Brown Jack ", 22
" Winnie Lass ", Ch., 22
" Linwhinny Ladybird ", 40
Literature of British Dogs, The, 2
" Little Brand ", Ch., 13, 21
" —— King ", 22
" —— Queen ", 22
" —— Sunray ", 13
Livre de Chasse, Le, 1
Lloyd, H. S., 15, 16, 18, 21, 26, 27, Pl. vi
" Lochar Smokey ", 42, 44
" Lovebird of Solway ", Ch., 25
Lynch, I. E., 44

" Mably Sharon ", 43
McDonald, David, 13, 21
Malarkey, J., 47
" Mallard of Glenbervie ", 41, 42, 45
Management, 66-72
Manifold, Miss J., 45

Manin, M., 44
Markham, Gervase, 2
" Marmion of Marmion ", Ch., 22
Mary, Queen, 2
Mason, G., 43, 47
" Matford Scamp ", 22
" —— Shot ", 22
" —— Sport ", 22
Mating, 56-58
Medicine Cupboard, 72
" Mellilotus Royal Oak ", Am. Ch., 33, Pl. x
"—— Shooting Star", Am. Ch., Pl. xv
M.E.S.S.S., 21, 27, 30, 31, 32, 34
Midgley, Mrs. Joan, 35, 42, 43, 47
——, Victor, 47
Millbank, Dr and Mrs. S., 14
" Millheugh Dainty Maid ", 37
" Mop I ", 3
Morgan, Dick, 31, 32, 36, 37
Morrel, J., 19
Morris, Lt-Col. L. H., 41
" Mowgrain Mr. Chips ", Ch., 35, 42, 43, 45, Pl. xiii
Muirhead family, 47
Musgrave, G. R., 29, 37, 39
" My Love of Bournview ", 37

Naisby, T., 29, 34
Name, Changes of, 7 , 17, 18
Nicolson, A. B., 34, 36, 38, 39, 40, 41, 42, 45
" Nimrod ", 9
" Nitro Powder ", 9
" Nobel Standard ", 23
Noisy dogs, 69, 70
" Noranby Rattle ", 23
" —— Rusty ", 23
Norfolk, Duke of, 4, 5
" Northdown Donna ", Ch., 44, 46, Pl. xi
" Northern Command ", 34
" Nuthill Dignity ", Ch., 22

Obedience work, 79-81
Of Englishe Dogges, 2
" Onyx of Stubham ", 44, 46
Otter in the bed, 19
Our Dogs, 74

"Painted Lady ", Ch., 35
Parks, F. W., 39
Parnell, J. J., 45
Parsons, Fred, 42
Patey, Mrs. H., 44
Patiala, H.H. the Maharajah of, 16
Peregrines, 19
" Peter of Lorton Fell ", Ch., 36, 38, 39, 40, 41, Pl. vii
" —— —— Shotton ", 32, 34
" Peter's Benefactor ", 29, 37, Pl. vii
Phillips, C. A., 7, 8, 11, 24
Picard, Pl. iv
" Pierrepont Brand ", 24
" —— Perfection ", 24
" —— Splint ", F.T. Ch., 24
Pike, Miss R., 21
" Pixie of Larkstoke ", 31
Placey, H. J., 21
" Pleasant Peter ", Ch., 29
Pointer, The, 6
Points, Scale of, 50
Portal, Lady, 21
Power, E. V., 34
Price, L. Turton, 13
" Pride of Abbotscross ", 40
" Prim of Ardrick ", 43
" Princess of Glenbervie ", 40
" Print of Ardrick ", Int. Ch., 41, 42, 43, 44, 45
Pug, 14
Pug Handbook, The, 14

Quadrupedibus, 2
Qualifying Certificate, 83
" Queen Mona of Solway ", 26

" Racedale Rover ", Pl. xvi
" Ranger of Ranscombe ", 24
" Rascal ", 24
Reast, Mrs. S., 41
Redlich, Mrs. Anna, 47
Registrations, 94-95
Reinagle, Pl. ii
" Reipple ", 24
" Renrut Beau ", 24

" Renrut Patsy ", 24
" —— Rose ", 24
" —— Rosery Brambletyke ", 24
" —— Tickie ", 24
Retriever, Flat-coated, 15
——, Golden, 23
——, Labrador, 14
" Reveller of Ranscombe ", 31
" Rex of Avendale ", F.T. Ch., 11, 13
Rickards, Dr. E., 31
Riddle, Maxwell, 53
" Rivington Don ", 24
" —— Meg ", 24
" —— Ringlet ", 24
" —— Rocket ", 24
" —— Rollo ", 24
" —— Sam ", F.T.Ch., 11
" Roan ", 24
Robinson, Miss Judith, 44, 46
" Rollick ", 24
" —— of Harting ", 18
" Romp ", 24
"Roundwood Haynford Lady ", 39
" —— Lass ", Ch., 25
" —— Remember ", 25
" —— Roger the Rake ", 35
" Royal Salute of Stubham ", Ch., 42, 43
" Rufton Recorder ", Ch., 25
" ——Ringmaster ", 25
" Rugby Lad ", 40

" St. Peter's Victoria ", Pl. vii
" Sam of Hagley ", 15
" Sandylands Shandy ", 35, 36, 37
" —— Sherry ", 33
" —— Shot ", 33, 34
" —— Showgirl ", 32, 33
" —— Shrubly ", Ch., 33, 34
" —— Soubranie ", 35, 42
" —— Starling ", 32
Sartorius, Pl. ii
Scott, Hon. George, 21, 22
——, G. R., 46
——, John, Pl. ii

Scottish Kennel Club, 13, 20
S.C.S., 51
Selby-Lowndes, Mrs. W., 18, 31
Senior, Mrs. D. M., 47
Setter, 4, 6
Sharpe, Isaac, 9
Shaw, Vera, Pl. v
Sheepdogs, Derbyshire, 15
Sherwood, Mrs. F., 44, 45
" Sheila of Stubham ", 39, 46, 55
Shoesmith, R. J., 26
Shooting, Pl. iii
Show preparation, 74, 75, 76
—— requisites, 76
" Showman of Shotton ", Int. Ch., 53, Pl. x
" Shultz ", 9
" Sidger ", 16
" Simon of Happeedaze ", 37
Size, 52, 53
" Skipper of Happeedaze ", 38
" Slick O'Vara " , 26
" Slip O'Vara ", 26
Smellie, G. H., 37
Smith, B., Pl. v
——, F. Winton, 7, 9, 16, Pl. vi
——, H. Winton, 7
——, Mrs. R. Gilman, 33
Smithson, Mrs. S., 37, 39, 40, 42, 43, 44, 45
" Solitaire of Happeedaze ", Ch. 33
Sowter, Mrs. A. T., 38, 42
' Spainel ', 1, Pl. i
Spaniel, Aqualate, 7, 9
——, Breton, Pl. iv
——, Cock, 5
——, Cocker, 3, 34, 44
——, O'Vara, Welsh, 7
——, Cocking, 2
——, Crouching, 2
——, English, 3
——, Field, 3, 7, 9
——, Irish Water, 26
——, Land, 2
——, Norfolk, 4, 7, Pls. iv, v
——, ' Perfectest ', 3
——, Springing, 2, 5
——, Sussex, 4, 5
——, Toy Black-and-Tan, 5
——, Water, 2, Pl. i

Spaniel, Welsh Springer, 7
—— Club, 6
' Spaynel ', 1
" Specialist ", 28
Spence, Mrs. T., 43
Sporting Spaniel, The, 7, 8
Sporting Spaniel Society, 6, 8
" Sprightly of Happeedaze ", Ch., 32, 33
" Springbok of Ware ", Ch., 18, 26, 27, Pl. vi
" Sportsman of Toton ", 28
" Staindrop Patricia ", F.T.Ch., 53
" Staitley May Queen ", 31, 34
" —— Skymaster ", 30
" —— Success ", 30
" —— Sunlight ", 30
" Stand Back ", 32
" Standard ", Ch., 16
Standard, The, 48-53
——, American, 51
" Starshine of Ide ", 31, 33
" Start of Happeedaze ", 32
Steen, Jan, 8
Stephenson, C. F., 47
Stevenson, E. E. A., 44, 45
" Stokeley Bonny Boy ", 34, 35, Pl. viii
" —— Falcon ", 44
" ——Flight ", 42
" —— Gay Boy ", Ch., 35, 39, Pl. xii
" —— Lucky ", Ch., 38, Pl. viii
" —— Sea Princess ", 41, 44
" —— Sprite ", 41, Pl. xiii
" Stonebrig Seraph ", 42
Stonex, Mrs. Elma, 23
" Strathblane Bonnie ", 35
" Stream O'Vara ", 26
Strickland, Miss O., 28
Stubbs, Pl. v
" Studley Annabelle ", 43
" —— Brave Buccaneer ", 40, 41, 42, 44, Pl. xii
" —— Diadem ", 45
" —— Dragoon ", 45
" —— Grenadier of Stubham ", 45
" —— Hercules ", Am. Ch., 40
" —— Major ", 39, 42
" Style O'Vara ", 26

" Sue of Amberside ", 31
" Susan of Stubham ", 38, 39, 55

Taylor, E. Lumb, 35
——, G. A., 16, 17, 30, 32, 34, 35, 39
" Tedwyns Tailfly ", 26
" —— Togs ", 26
" —— —Trex ", 17, 26
" —— Trick ", 26
Temper (Never lose it!), 82
Temperament, 51
Temperature, 70
Tetton, Poem to, 10
Thomas, R. G., 38, 42
Thompson, Mrs. Frank, 37
Thomson, Mrs. Gertrude, 28
" Thoughtful of Harting ", Dual Ch., 18
Tiercel, 19
Till, Mrs. F. Oughtred, 38, 39, 40, 43, 45, 46
——, Mr. and Mrs. S. H., 25, 35, 39, 45, 46
" Tillan Toddy ", 37, 38
" Timperley Beauty ", 26
" —— Gun Master ", 26
" —— Topper ", 26
" Tissington Flush ", 3, 4, Pl. v
" Totonian Belle ", 35
" —— Biddy ", 36
" —— Comet ", 39
" —— Finder ", 28
Traherne, Capt. O. P., 16, 23
Training, 78-84
Travers, Mr. and Mrs., 28, 35, 36, 39
Trimble, Ernest, 22, 32
" Tring ", 11
Trotter, A. L., 17
" Trout O'Vara ", 26
Turberville, 2
Turner, Miss F. L., 24

" Vanity Fair of Stubham ", Sh. Ch., 45, Pl. xiii
" Velox Powder ", F . T . Ch., 9

Wachtelhund, Pl. iv

Warnes, A. G., 47
Warwick, B. J., 6
Wasp sting, Fatal, 29
Waterhouse, Mr. and Mrs. F., 47
Watkinson, Mrs. D., 47
Watts, C., 9
Weaning, 63
Wearne, E., 47
Webster, J. S., 43
Wells, Ernest, 11
——, Dr. W. G. P., 47
" Whaddon Chase Bonny Lass ", 38
" —— —— —— Tom ", Ch., 31, 33, 34
" —— —— Bracken ", Ch., 34, 35
" —— —— Destiny ", 44
" —— —— Grouse ", 39
" —— —— Primula ", 36
" —— —— Prince ", Ch., 35, 36, 37
" —— —— Romance ", 39
" —— —— Salote ", 41, 44
" —— —— Snipe ", 33, 34
" —— —— Swift ", 39
" —— —— Titch ", 33
Whelping, 59-61
—— chart, 95
—— signs, 59
" Whintonhill Raider ", 44
" —— Tessa ", 34, 35, 44
Wilkins, Miss Joan, 37
——, Miss M. E., 47
William the Conqueror, 20
Williams, D. J., 47
——, J., 43
——, Mrs. Maureen, 47
" Winch Agate ", 36
" Winning Number of Solway ", Ch., 25
Witch-hazel, 71, 72
Withers, M. D., 28
" Wollburn Wallflower ", 39, 41, Pl. ix
" —— Wattie Honey ", 39
Woodham, E. C., 47
Woods, Mrs. M., 43
" Woodsorrel Jenny Wren ", 43
Worms, 56, 58
Wright, Mrs. M., 47